New Hope for the Dead

# New Hope for the Dead
## Uncollected William Matthews

Edited by

Sebastian Matthews & Stanley Plumly

Red Hen Press | Pasadena, CA

*New Hope for the Dead*
Copyright © 2010 by Sebastian Matthews and Stanley Plumly
All rights reserved

No part of this book may be used or reproduced in any manner whatsoever without the prior written permission of both the publisher and the copyright owner.

Book layout by Elizabeth Davis
Book design by Mark E. Cull

Matthews, William, 1942 – 1997.
  New hope for the dead: uncollected William Matthews / edited by Sebastian Matthews & Stanley Plumly.—1st ed.
     p. cm.
  Poems, stories, essays, reviews, letters, interviews.
  ISBN 978-1-59709-162-6
  I. Matthews, Sebastian, 1965- II. Plumly, Stanley. III. Title.
  PS3563.A855N48 2010
  818'.54—dc22
                            2010032328

The Annenberg Foundation, the James Irvine Foundation, the Los Angeles County Arts Commission, The City of Los Angeles Department of Cultural Affairs, California Arts Council, and the National Endowment for the Arts partially support Red Hen Press.

First Edition

Published by Red Hen Press
Pasadena, CA
www.redhen.org

# Acknowledgements

I would like to thank those who have helped me with this project and last decade of executor work. Stanley Plumly, of course, my coeditor through it all. It's not possible to convey here all the important and subtle things Stan has taught me along the way.

To Russell Banks and Chase Twichell for being mentors, my literary uncle and aunts. And to my father's other friends, especially Marvin & Dorothy Bell, Sharon Bryan, Christopher Buckley and Dan Halpern. Thanks to Tony Hoagland for understanding so well.

To Michael Collier at Houghton Mifflin for working with me, Stan and Peter Davison on putting out *Search Party*, and for being such an amazing force in all our literary lives. To Stephen Corey at *Georgia Review* for his intelligent editing work on the Matthews-Banks-Plumly-Halpern correspondence. To Ted Genoways for publishing both my and my father's work in the amazing *Virginia Quarterly Review*. To Richard Jackson for his sharp editing on the Horace translation at Au Sable Press & to Chase Twichell for publishing it. & to Edward Bryne for all his fine work as writer and editor.

To Sascha Feinstein for editing a wonderful Matthews tribute in *Brilliant Corners: A Journal of Jazz & Literature*. To Chad Oness and his creative team at Sutton Hoo Press for the beautiful work on *Provisions*, their stunning letterpress edition of my father's prose and prose poems. & to Cris Cristafaro for providing the amazing art work for the edition. To Keith Flynn at *Asheville Poetry Review* for all the small and large things he does for the cause. To the folks who put together *Blues for Bill: A Tribute to William Matthews*—Ken Brown, Meg Kearney, Donna Reis and Estha Weiner. To Estha Weiner for hosting 10 years of William Matthews Memorial Readings at City College of New York. To Gary Clark at Vermont Studio Center for his help in creating the short-lived but important William Matthews Prize. & to the folks at Lily Library for housing his literary archive.

Thanks also to Susan Matthews and Mary Matthews, along with loads of love. To Ali and Avery, of course, and Marie Harris and Charter Weeks, our senseis. To Brother Bill, my silent partner. To Dr. Lawrence & Diane Climo. To August Venturini for all his help, both legal and personal. In memory of Peter Davison and Carol Houck Smith.

I'd like to thank Kate Gale and Mark E. Cull (& the staff at Red Hen Press!) for putting this book together and hatching it out into the world. This was fun, start to finish.

Thanks go to the editors of the following journals and reviews in which many of these pieces orginally appeared: *American Poetry Review, Asheville Poetry Review, Blackbird, Brilliant Corners, Georgia Review, New Yorker, Ohio Review, Poetry Interantional, Prairie Schooner, Valiporosa Review* & *Virginia Quarterly Review*.

# Contents

*Notes on Curating* Uncollected Matthews:
   An Introduction     xi

## *Poems*
   Rules That Brought Me Here     3
   More Snow     4
   Insomnia Again     6
   The Drunken Baker     7
   Matins     8
   Above the Aquarius Mine, Ward, Colorado     9
   Dancing to Reggae Music     10
   Soccer Match, St. George, Bermuda     12
   Dylan and the Band, Boston Gardens, 1974     14
   Wild Horses on Ocracoke Island, North Carolina     15
   A Bedroom in the Basement     16
   Secretive     17
   Heedless     18
   Lonely     19
   Real     20
   WKU 17598     22
   A Blessing from Texas     24
   Last Words     26
   Inheritance Tax     28
   The Inventions of Memory     31
   Clearwater Beach, Florida, 1950     32
   Brief Farewells     34
   Office Life     35
   The Spokesman     36
   A Diner     37
   No     38

| | |
|---|---|
| Smart Money | 40 |
| Sentence | 41 |
| The Dogs of Monotone at Dusk | 42 |
| Dazzle | 43 |
| Keep A-Knockin' | 44 |
| The Village Vanguard | 45 |
| A Citizen | 46 |
| The Holiday Inn/Scope, | |
|     Norfolk, Virginia, Spring, 1980 | 47 |
| Television and Piqua, Ohio | 48 |
| Moshe Dor, Country | 50 |
| Out | 52 |
| Sad Stories Told in Bars: The Reader's Digest Version | 53 |

## *Stories*

| | |
|---|---|
| Growing Old | 57 |
| Nessun Dorma | 60 |
| Blue Streak | 64 |
| Blues 52 | 67 |
| Doc Holliday's Grave | 70 |
| One Close Escape After Another | 74 |

## *Essays*

| | |
|---|---|
| The Poetry I Want | 79 |
| On Reviewing | 80 |
| Two Takes on Richard Hugo | 82 |
| A Night at the White House | 85 |

What It Means to Be American:
    Emily Dickinson's Home Economics    90
Martial's Darts    94
Shortages    105
Poetic License    115

*Reviews*
    William Stafford's Whetstone    127
    Dignity from Head to Toe    130
    On Tony Hoagland's *Donkey Gospel*    139

*Letters*
    Peripheral Pleasures: Letters to Russell Banks,
        Daniel Halpern *&* Stanley Plumly
        (with an Introduction by Sebastian Matthews)    145

*Interviews*
    Living by the Long River:
        Excerpts from Interviews—Early, Middle & Late    193

*Miscellany*
    Last Lines:
        A Commonplace Book Constructed After the Fact    223

*Afterword*
    "To Learn to Love the Blues": Edward Byrne    227

Photo by Star Black   Photo by Ted Rosenberg

# *Notes on Curating* Uncollected Matthews: An Introduction

In jazz, as in the "Po Biz," originality and tone carry the utmost importance. You either sing or you talk. Your words are plain-spoken or fly in an aviary of language; you look back to your forefathers or you forge ahead in the *avant garde*. Of course, the greats find a way to do it all; over a career, they keep transforming from one incarnation into some other new startling hybrid.

There's an apocryphal story of saxophonist Lester Young in which he is hiding away in a hotel room overlooking Birdland, drinking himself to death, listening down on the pale versions of his sound night after night. By the time he was thirty, Charlie Parker had so many imitators he could barely take a step forward without running into himself. You can hear Coltrane every night on jazz stages around the globe. There comes a point when all innovators get copied to such an extent that the originality of his or her work comes into question. People begin to accept the imitation as the original, may even forget the original altogether.

To some degree, this fate threatens to befall William Matthews and his ouervre. One reviewer, set on discrediting his importance as a poet, argued that Matthews had no particular voice or style. There are a good many intelligent criticisms of my father's work, but that is not one of them. It's no offense to Billy Collins to say that when he first started publishing poems they sounded a lot like Matthews. Or that there are two generations of poets who have been freed by my father's later work to speak in a voice rich enough to include personal life alongside erudite musings, and to fit a quirky, urbane *patois* into tight, lyrical lines. Tony Hoagland says it well—about both Matthews and Larry Levis—when he calls their life works "promontories in the landscape that survives them."

But defense is not my job here. Matthews' *Search Party: Collected Poems* can fend for itself. (It doesn't hurt that *Search Party* was a finalist for the Pulitzer Prize.) With *New Hope for the Dead*, Stanley Plumly and I hope to celebrate Matthews' already rich voice by deepening and widening it—including more uncollected poems along with a selection of short stories, essays, articles, letters and interviews. With this collection, we hope to alter the reader's sense of William Matthews' legacy by capturing, as three-dimensionally as we can, my father's full range as a man and writer—cook, lover of wine and music, friend, critic, thinker, wit, commentator and citizen, translator, teacher, colleague.

In doing so, we will be rounding out what my father started with *Curiosities* (University of Michigan Press, 1989) and we continued with *The Poetry Blues: Essays & Interviews of Williams Matthews* (University of Michigan Press, 2001). We also find ourselves completing our own trio of co-edited collections, starting with *Poetry Blues* and moving to *Search Party* (Houghton Mifflin, 2004) on through to this book—a decade of collaborative work capped.

---

*New Hope for the Dead* starts off with the last of Matthews' uncollected poems. We selected this group of nearly 40 poems out of a stack of over 200, choosing poems from all stages of Matthews' career, early to late. We then picked about half the short stories published in journals such as *Ohio Review* and *New England Review*. It came as a surprise to realize my father had been writing short fiction for over twenty years; like the poets Mark Strand and Larry Levis, Matthews had both an ear and an eye for the form.

The remaining top-shelf essays, articles and reviews come next, including an unpublished account of a grand poets' dinner at President Jimmy Carter's White House and a cooking article first published in *The New York Times*, complete with a set of recipes. In his reviews and essays about reviewing, Matthews returns to his pet subjects—translating Martial, language, domestic life, the work of his friends. The last piece we include here is of Tony Hoagland's *Donkey Gospel*, a book my father helped select for the 1997 James McLaughlin Award of the Academy of American Poets.

Originally published in one of *The Georgia Review*'s correspondence issues, "Peripheral Pleasures" is collection of letters my father wrote to his close friends and writing buddies Russell Banks, Dan Halpern and Stanley Plumly. The selection opens with a brief introduction that attempts to place my father's correspondence inside his larger body of work. Next come interview excerpts from nearly a dozen interviews spanning Matthews' career. Fittingly, the book ends with Edward Byrne's thorough and generous essay on my father's poetic legacy.

The title of the book comes from one of my father's one-liners, most famously collected in his 1971 mini chapbook, *An Oar in the Old Water*. The poem was made into a bumpersticker back in the 70s by The Alternate Press.

A while back I was walking with a long-time friend and poetry pal, enjoying one of our rare face to face visits. We were talking about my father's death and the executor work I'd been doing. She thought that my writing the memoir and collecting his poems was more than a labor of love but also a way to move through a syndrome. I needed to get past my father, in many ways a "pain in the neck" legacy. She was right, of course, but there's more to it. For, in a sense, the very work I've been undertaking has kept my father in my life. I have both moved past him and remain utterly intertwined with him. In an article for *Poets & Writers* I used the metaphor of tending a garden. This image has only deepened. As with any garden, I keep coming back to work the soil. The money I receive from my father's royalty checks helps pay for the literary journal I coedit. I continue to grant permissions, participate in memorials, gather material for his archives, write essays about his work, etc.

Because I live up in the mountains of Western North Carolina, I find myself surrounded by my father's old friends. Some of his oldest friends live here, or just down the mountain in Chapel Hill, my unlikely birthplace. Other friends arrive in town for readings—Coleman Barks, Marvin Bell, Fred Chappell, Robert Morgan, Quincy Troupe. Even my cohost for a local poetry radio show once served as a student intern for *Lillabulero*, the literary journal my father founded with novelist Russell Banks. I receive letters and packages every few weeks with old poems, tapes of recordings, old postcards penned by my father.

I encounter former students about a dozen times a year—on email, if you can call that an encounter, or in person—and almost always enjoy hearing the old stories. Recently I received a letter from a poet who had been a student of my father's. What made this poet's letter special was a transcribed list of my father's teaching advice—a cobbled philosophy of tips on writing poetry taken as notes in a class held thirty years ago. In his brief note, the poet writes, "About half the time we'd get together to discuss my work, he didn't want to talk poetry at all, preferring instead to talk jazz, basketball or even baseball. Somehow I figured out these 'non-poetry' poetry sessions were important to him, where he could just be himself so I didn't bring up that week's poems I'd turned in. The other half of the time he'd go over my work. What follows is his advice (some of the best I've ever had) mostly as I wrote it down."

Here are the notes the poet took, slightly altered to avoid confusion:

1. Who speaks affects tone.
2. A false audience leads to false habits.
3. Don't look over your shoulder too much.
4. Don't be too careful not to travel in your poems.
5. Technique has consequences.
6. Is your first stanza doing work or is it a "pre-echo" of what's to come?
7. Find a way to talk about what interests you.
8. Watch out for big words that slang hasn't caught up to.
9. Be careful of being on your best behavior. Tentative rhythm equals tentative thinking.
10. The ear is related to your best thinking; your best thinking equals your best confidence.

It's a boon of letter, of course, as though I have been handed a time capsule of my father dug up from the academic bone yard.

The poet has his favorites, and so do I. For me, number 1 speaks loudly, 3 cracks a joke and 5 gives us a wry but slightly ominous warning. On first read, the list feels like a perfect summation of a lecture to beginners. But, on second and third reading, it feels more like the list a pro tapes above the desk to remember the essentials. The letter ends: "He always wanted the best for his students and their best poems from them too."

If this book works at all, it does so by bringing my father briefly back to life, as lit up as when reading well, running a lively workshop or laughing with friends over good food and glasses of wine.

*Sebastian Matthews*

# New Hope for the Dead

# POEMS

# Rules That Brought Me Here

If it helps you to sleep, you had better learn to love it.

Reason seeks its own defeat. Take the case of N. "There are two alternatives," he would say. Then they both came to him in a dream—twin succubi—and since everything seemed possible in dreams he invented a second N for the duration. You can guess what happened. For a while the three of them pretended N would come back. Later they drifted apart. The one with the mole on her hip became a dancer, the other a hot-tongued dental assistant. The second N went "home" to N's wife and was forgiven.

Fables are true. They go on happening. Once a lady in Texas saw on her TV the test pattern of a station 14 years defunct. Definitions of "reality" are stupid. Here we are.

Tragedy is good for you, but it hurts. Tell them you gave at the office. Then lock yourself in your room and give, in silence, to yourself.

When it is fully beautiful, it is finished. Then you must leave it. Before naming whatever place you reach when you stop leaving it, remember everything I've told you.

# More Snow

By breakfast the snow was two feet deep.
The shovel would fill with snow from the air
before I could pry
at the driveway, and anyway
the radio said the roads
were ramps to the ditches,
no work, no school
and the hiss of snow falling
as if onto a fire.

In the morning, more snow.
On the window, a membrane
of frost. The children kept falling asleep.
Phone lines snapped like guitar strings.
Looking through the frost
we thought the earth was underwater.
Nothing big swam by, but snowy
plankton sifted to the rising bottom.

Next day I found gray clumps of frost
just under my skin, like lice.
Snow shifted on the sagging roof.
The children were sick of soup.
I read them a story
until the drifting snow
had covered the highest line of type
and the story fell asleep.

Next morning the bathtub was full
of snow. Between bulletins
the radio broadcast the President breathing.
More snow and no bread.
When I cracked an egg
a ribbon of snow uncoiled.
We slept in our flesh
like nomads in cumbersome tents.
Snow filled our dreaming skulls
with the music of mutes.

At dawn it stopped. We woke
to the gurgling bathtub and radio
and tumbled from windows
to dig our doorways out.
Birds bloomed weakly in the trees,
heavy-winged and hungry.
I still wear in my nose
the spoor left by the snow.
But all that day the sun swung
in the sky like an udder
and everyone on the blank lawns
mooed and danced
and ate handfuls of snow.

# Insomnia Again

It's Lord Anguish up late in his robe. The loose cinch flicks, a little plaid dog, at his heels. *There's not enough water in snow to save a man from dying of thirst*, he tells the drifts of correspondence on his desk.

It is important to ground your life: then, you can no longer use the words "my life" as an abstract (from the Latin for "withdraw") noun. *I feel like Los Angeles*, he says.

It will be harder to resolve this fugue of lucid fuss than to pass through the eye of a hurricane. The other cheek stings too. On the one hand, there is the other hand, a toad made of knuckles.

He passes his desk like a scratch in a record returning to the needle. He begins whistling something trite but, somehow, poignant. That's what the old songs are for, that's why I do this, that's why we listen. *Good night*, we are saying to each other, *sweet dreams*.

# The Drunken Baker

Those pale fish, his hands—
he never thinks of them: what good
are married daughters?

Three days he's been like this.
They shape his every
loaf of breath.

# Matins

Tell yourself that love points only to the tip of its own needle. Go in that direction until you are dusty with fatigue and God's bees won't come. Lift your sticky voice. Tell yourself your name again and again until it sounds like a lost prayer.

# Above the Aquarius Mine, Ward, Colorado

My dog clatters up a talus pile. Is there a key-stone, that when he steps on it will organize a slide? The thin air hasn't got to him yet. He pranks down toward us, stiff in his forelegs but his head's not back, it's jutted toward us and his tail goes in circle like a pump-handle, he's dancing as if there'll always be enough water, enough air.

We trudge up a swale, happy, 9500 feet. Locusts clack past. One makes its first stroke just as it passes my ear: it sounds like a bowstring let go.

As we near the ridge the view drops away. We go out onto a promontory and stare over the trough. Just as I turn to go back down, a locust, going the other way, loops over my shoulder, over the edge. My dog's so tired he slinks back down. He looks as if he's claimed this place in the name of something he's ashamed of, now that he's done it, but he's only tired and keeping close to the ground, wherever it goes.

# Dancing to Reggae Music

The night, with its close breath
of sawdust and overproof rum,
its clatter of waxy leaves above
this scuff of earth we print
and erase—the night pours
over us its star-spotted syrup
of wakefulness. I love the halt
and stutter both, and the lyrics
with their exultant certainties
about politics and religion:
*I want to disturb my neighbor
'cause I'm feeling so right.*

Somebody's lit a spliff, I can tell
by the dense caramel of ganja smoke.
There are trances of paying
attention, and trances of giving
it up, which is where the blue-
grey ganja smoke will go, slowly,
it's so thick and layered,
and where the scent of dancing
will go, a little acrid the way
an armpit is after orgasm,
as if acrid meant truculent
to come back to our common life
after the trances of the self

we use each other for.
How easy it is to dance about
the self, and easy to confuse
it with the constellate body.
If they were the same, we couldn't
move, much less dance the night
away that's leaving us anyhow.
It too will go up, pushed back
by the salt light of dawn coming
from the ocean. And up is where
we go from here, after a detour
through dust. *So long, politics
and religion. Hello, stars.*

# Soccer Match, St. George, Bermuda

These are the Christmas winds,
a high surf in the air. For weeks
the weather is moody, except
underwater: the usual
thick hush, and at the surface
breath rising and falling
in snorkels, a dull and
beautiful music. But nobody's
diving today. The winds flare
to fifty knots, gale force,
and blow east goal to west.
Each side's slammed onto attack
for half the match. Finally
a tall mid-fielder, so black
he looks purple, like an iris,
scores from thirty yards.
The goalie tries to fist it out
but it blurs past him,
wobbling fast. The rest of the match
he screams for his teammates
to be good, but they can only
hear him a few yards. Wind rips
his words back like a scarf
blown straight out behind him
and he's alone, rapt in his urges.
The rain from the Azores
comes in so horizontal

it skids across the field.
There's a blue glow in the goalie's
face from yelling. His team
beats the ball upwind and never scores.

## Dylan and the Band, Boston Gardens, 1974

They're pros. They start on time,
one sentence of patter, no subject,
*glad to be back in Boston*, then
they play. Every song we want
to be an anthem, Dylan sings
violently different from the way
he recorded it, as if he means
to outlive his prophecies
that came true and especially
those that didn't. *How does it feel?*
he gloats and everyone roars
but none of us knows. It feels
like an epidemic of music,
how music infects disbelief
and how that makes us happy,
even those of us onstage, and so
he says *See you next year*
and next year he doesn't
come back, nor the Band, nor do we.

# Wild Horses on Ocracoke Island, North Carolina

The paper placemats
in the restaurants
advertise
Wild Ponies.
Driving along Route 12,
you can see them running
not quite wild, for the sea
on one side & fences on three others
keep them in, making them
good neighbors.

Fences also keep the tourists out.
Otherwise some drunk
                          & self-
anointed cowboy would one day
lurch in, yodeling,
the wife & kids back in the car
aghast at Silly Daddy.

And, too, the residents need never
fear the night a horse
is found
        inside the house
& who knows what secret rider
come in from the sea
waiting in the yard.

# A Bedroom in the Basement

If our bed was thin and we were
together barely half a fat person,
we were enough. The way a convict
learns law, that's how we studied
each other's ambiguous bodies,
skeptical, like good scholars.
From its one high lawn-level window
the half-buried room would begin
at dawn to sift itself into grey
sooty light. We were exhausted.
Everything we fed each other was meant
to be unforgettable, and suppose
it was. This is how we fall in love,
and where. Over our heads, inside
our slack and cagey bodies, in sleep.
Sleep is no balm to hurt minds. The hurt
mind dreams, the debts of memory
gather, and any mind is meant to work
and so be strained. In sleep the body
is free from any prurience but its own,
except this one: I dream we're sleeping.
You can do it, too. We lie in our skinny
bodies on the dewy lawn and watch our
skinny bodies sleep in the brightening room.

## Secretive

Low clouds, gray rain, a lifetime
of Sundays, nothing but small talk

to talk. Think how dull straight-
lined life could be, except that we make

paths from our digressions, and from
our paths, stories, and from those,

our lives. A few details gather
to these stories, like eager pets,

but for each of them a hundred
are misremembered, or erased,

as if to leave our children room
for anecdotes. And what will they tell?

Story after story
about memory itself.

# Heedless

Years later she'd tell anyone who knew
them both how she and he had lived a year
together, and then he'd had a—here
she'd enunciate—*nervous breakdown*
when she refused to marry him.

None of this true. It made him dark with shame,
not to have known her then but to be bland
now while she still bore her acid passion
like a souvenir. It seems another life,
he'd muse, not thinking how one night he'd toured
his house, throwing on all the lights until
anywhere he looked was blare. And he lay down
and closed his eyes and everything was still
light, shadowless light, and a new woman.

Breath held its breath, the passive voice strode in,
and the sentence carried itself out.
Love fell on them like stars in Alabama.
Beware the speed of verbs. They got involved,
were seen together, seeing each other.
They were stories and told them to them-
selves, though after those exactions, and soon,
when they rose a last time from bed, they left
them there, like uncorrected proofs, almost
as if to have something besides themselves,
some testament, to be unfaithful to.

# Lonely

This is the same darkness we'll all
lazily describe as "falling," we're so
carelessly happy in our porch chairs
at dusk, all in agreement like shoes
on the closet floor. Soon it will be
dispersed equally everywhere and out
of it our bodiless voices will rasp:
how different we are from each other after all,
we remember as the separateness of sleep
begins to spread in us like so many dusks.

*Articulation*, we call it, but what
we break into breath gets compressed
and redistributed by dreams, by sleep's hum,
by the consonantal slur of the slack body.
But this is what refreshes us.
It's for this that we cry "good night,
good night," and mate with ourselves
in sleep. And then we wake, eager for talk.
We agree to meet on the porch around five,
and all of us arrive a little early.

# Real

In *Five Easy Pieces*, Nicholson doesn't exactly
return from LA: suddenly he is twirling
Sally Struthers, a mad carnie whirligig,
the machine taking itself for a ride.
She's frantic sounding, wolfing air
like nausea, but the listener needs time
to hear a rhythm, and hers is the gasp
of striving, running awkward into the wind
like a drawing-board angel, and the wind
helps with gaining force—or her rush
is the rising wind. Hers is not anxiety
to jump free of the spinning, but a scramble
to lift on what resists her orgasm. Having
kicked loose, she settles, or she rises. She comes.

It is a dizzying thing to watch with no warning,
for our silent protagonist too, I think—that's
the point of the jump-cut: suddenly you are spinning,
your cock like the cable with which a boy
tethers a model plane's buzzing circles around him.
Vertigo is the body's moral of any story
in which you are the center of the world,
but you are showing off, fucking on your feet—
though the ground tips, rising and falling
like an animal that would fling you off,
you can catch that rhythm, take its air
and breath as your own and praise it,
till it eats from your hand and likes being ridden.

Besides, the little engine soon enough runs
out of fuel, the woman is thrown off and
she subsides into space.
He bends to place her body on the bed
where lesser men make the world flat,
places her down like a brass plate on the shore.
In large letters it proclaims, "This land is
true and it is mine, thus says King Stud."
Were it not for his face beaming its
boyish "Now tell me that wasn't something,"
you would believe the world is real.

# WKU 17598

*stenciled on a bed (mine for five nights in March, 1984) at the guest house, Western Kentucky University, Bowling Green, Kentucky*

Finally our common wealth may be a list,
and here where the current president
of WKU slept the night before his interview,
where James Dickey may sleep this week-
end and Howard Norman the next,
and then the next an assistant professor
of sociology (trim beard, grey
herringbone coat and a cottonmouth
yawning with jargon?), I lay me down to sleep
and to dream and to scuffle across the hall
at 5:00 am to pee, to lower my umber line
and to reel it back in dry and erased
by itself, and to lie back down to bob
like a moored boat for two more hours.

That's what I thought at 5:00 am, but
while rain shinnied down rain outside
my window I slept until 9 as snugly
as *The Maid of the Mist* behind
the demure curtains of Niagara Falls.
And when I woke it was too late
for something I'd need to name
in order fully to miss it. The agenda
of forgetting, too, is a list as if to give
is to receive the absence of the given.
Poems tumble from the top of the page,

the top of my head, tip of my tongue,
but the mist rises like memory—
erasures, sleep, the onionskin of breath
and showersteam that I smear
clear every morning to shave.

The sociologist is 5'3" and lectured
on confusions between love and work,
austere in her chalky suit and pearly
in her blouse—grizzled peach in color,
severely cut, effulgent at her lecturing
throat. By then I was in Bowling
Green, Ohio. Like anywhere in America,
it was almost home. In the Falcon
Crest Motel in Bowling Green, Ohio,
home of the 1984 NCAA Division I
ice hockey champions, I lay myself
down and slept and woke and made
when I woke a list of things to do
and then I did them, one by one
and all in their inertial weight by all.

# A Blessing from Texas

It's a usual day in Houston,
dank on the delta floor and hot.
I watch the clouds conflate, tuft on
tuft and curd on curd—the city of God
conducting its business without us,
our longing, our cumulus of pride
and heartbreak, our eloquent soliloquies
about being lonely, each of us,

as a cloud. This is a notion the Gulf-
bound clouds ceremoniously leaving Houston
would find ludicrous, if they didn't spend
their massed senses of humor imitating
the long, slow dumb show of matter—
here a pig, there a juniper, and there
a lobster with a broken claw.
And out to sea they ceaselessly go.

Though change is no religion to them,
for religion lives by lack. Think how a great
love too readily met can slacken itself
in such swift happiness and never break
through to the pain that breaks us to make
us whole, to a distillate maturity,
like an herb's, more piercingly exact
for having such a long, hard time

of itself. Off Galveston they're blessing
the shrimp fleet today, sprinkling holy
water onto the waters. I'd bless you
if you were here, my love, and instead
I wave my firm hand at the disappearing
clouds. Go, I could be wishing them,
and look, they go. This magic is easy.
Who's blessing the shrimp? Oh, the British

bless the fox before the hunt, but that's
no blessing, it's an exculpation,
like the phone call the jilter makes
to see if the jiltee is alright, please.
To bless is to wound and to sever
(those slashes the Bishop of Galveston
makes in the unresisting air are a cross
because we know they are a cross).

*God love you*, we say when we won't.
Did I say my hand was firm? I lied.
To bless is also to relax one's hand.
Clouds scull overhead. Shrimpers bob
out onto the Gulf. If I turn my palms
down, will your absence fall away?
That's why we call them lifelines.
If this is choice, I take it. Bless, bless.

# Last Words

> Vae, puto deus fio. *(Alas, I suppose I am becoming a god.)*
> —*The Emperor Vespasian*

What needs to be said is fog,
or the billows of anesthesia,
or each sprig on a juniper
leaping into focus as anesthesia

burns off by body heat, by time,
by that half-life of flesh
which is only an idea but for flesh.
What needs to be said is all

vowels, or all consonants, I can't
remember which. Someone I love
is dying and I notice that *rage*
and *anger* are almost anagrams,

except for the sinister *n*, peak
and valley both. Hang on, don't go,
I'll think of what needs to be said.
Life, put words in my mouth.

The wafer is fog and salt and air
but the wafer is not words.
The wafer is the body of cardboard
sliced thin, but anyone's body

aspires to fog in one direction
and leafmold in another, as if
mixed feelings were a religion,
and doubt, and delay, and the speed

of time. I don't know what to say.
The electric typewriter purrs,
and the phone and phonograph
sputter tinily with surface noise,

like a poem or eulogy. *Deep*, we like
to say, and *between the lines*, and
*moving*. But here we stand on the surface
of our stammering lives, and dumb.

# Inheritance Tax

Men drift with flashlights,
copying from tombstones names
for the registration rolls.
They change some names: nobody's
called Jedediah anymore.
And they don't use anyone dead
after 1800: I once shook hands
with a woman who knew a man
who knew Meriwether Lewis (1774 –
1809). And why shouldn't the dead
vote? One euphemism for "to die"
is "to join the majority,"
except there are now more of us
alive than ever have been dead.
I don't know what this means
but it can't be good. If
history were a democracy, the dead
should be able to outvote us.
But the dead just lie there,
like the senior poor, in state,
and if we give everything to the poor
they are the rich and damned
by their sudden comfort, and
we're tenant farmers whose crop
is novice landlords.
Since Vietnam slang came home
we like to say that so-and-so bought

the farm, i.e., the gravesite,
the atom of real estate.
Whatever it is, this "everything,"
we leave it to our children, who live
despite our barrage of gifts
in another and several world:
in the child's drawing
the barn and genial pig
are the same size, and there's
a tiny man beside the barn,
as if for scale, like a tourist's
wife at the foot of a redwood.
The sun is tethered by one fiery
ray to a hair on the pig's right ear,
an antenna. If only we could
translate what the sun broadcasts,
its urgent crackle. We dance to it
anyway we can. Some mornings
at 5:00 even the milk-gorged Holsteins
aslosh in their stalls seem
to be dancing placidly, though
the only music you can hear
in the barn is the old
cracked-speaker Philco lisping
commodity prices from Chicago.
And what kind of dance does Laneta

do, down the road, at six kicked
stupid by a mare and living forty
years longer than anyone hoped,
pure and opaque in spirit as a turkey?
Every school day each of those years
she would stay home and watch the schoolbus come
and go, like an egg carton on wheels,
slow for the ruts in the road and take
our jiggling children off to their
dwindling and beautiful futures.

# The Inventions of Memory

Blue-black, the ink we squandered
for Penmanship was called,
and now, 5:00 a.m. in April,
twenty-eight years later,
the indelible sky is blue-
black for the same few
minutes birds begin to chitter
like a forming sentence.
There could be a blurt over there,
and a gurgle here, or even
(funny coincidence) both.
But once that hum, which by itself
would be a kind of dial-tone,
is added to the patois, then
something is stuttering over
the end of itself like a stone
skipped over water. How full
the voice is just before silence,
in which we can hear how the hum
is gone, and the gurgle and blurt;
now even the birds are quiet
and the light escaped from description,
since it's already dawn
and the grammar of memory
is rapt by its calisthenics,
its conversion of bruises to stories
about the dominion of bruises.

# Clearwater Beach, Florida, 1950

Each dockpost comes with a pelican
who seems to my eight-year-old eye
to be a very distinguished bat. And then
one languidly unrumples itself and flies
off like a purposeful overcoat.

Signs on the causeway warn not to eat
the oleander leaves. A new place means
new poisons. And the palmetto grass,
and the topknotted bromeliads, and
the jellyfish like clouds of clear brains

trailing rain. . . . The scenery is in another
language and I'm still besotted by
my own, half books and half Ohio.
A children's work is never done, so
I'm up early, stubbing my whole foot

on the sprinkler caps in the rosetted
grass. Is it too early to cry? Do I talk
too much? What does it mean to be full
of yourself, or on vacation?
There's something from church—a living

coal on the tongue—I remember. What's
a dead coal? It won't be breakfast
until the grown-ups break the blur and crust
of sleep and come downstairs, and al-
ready, once again, I'm given to language.

Though how could they have saved me?
I'm staunch in the light-blanched yard
and they're in sleep, through which their last
dreams of the morning drain,
and I'm in the small fort of my sunburnt body.

## Brief Farewells

Past blue farms shading gray
our taxi muttered grumpily.
For longer than it took to pass them,
I loved each barn, each stone, each vast-
eyed sleepy cow, each cold mailbox
with its metal flag alongside
like an oar. It's company
that fills the heart, the part of the heart
in charge of departure would say,
slamming shut its valves about to open
again so violently we'll hardly know
what sort of metaphor "heart attack"
is—a normal persistence
unopposed, a love gone wrong,
the ultimate inside job?
By the time we know how to begin
thinking about all this, we'll be
at the airport, splitting the fare,
hugs and kisses, terse waves, hands
about to close into baggage—
carrying fists, the very ground dense
in its unwillingness to fly with us.

# Office Life

Drab bickering, the empire dead and tax
reports alive, paperwork, erasure,
the grime on the philodendron leaves
since who tends everybody's plant?
It's the triumph of habit over appetite,
like comparing the stars to diamonds.
We make copies. We send out for food. Food
arrives. We have spats and tizzies and huffs.
Isn't it great being grown up, having
a job? We get our work done more or less
and go home. How was it today? we're asked
and don't know what to say. It's like wet soot,
like us, like what we feel: stuck on itself,
as, from here, starlight seems stuck to its star.

# The Spokesman

My father, dead for two months when I had
the dream, sat at the end, or head, I should
say, of the picnic table, and the rest
of us leaned across it, like happy extras
in an opera, and talked and had fun.
It was mid-afternoon in April and light
without glare or shadow bathed us all.
I like to think we knew that though he spoke
and toasted us each by name, he was dead.
And anyway I had the gift of fire
and let it kindle me, and I spoke:
*If he's not dead*, I said, and I could feel
the sentence I composed become an arrow—
its dowelled shaft, its milled tip, its fletch—and I
let it go. . . . *If he's not dead, why do we
have to bear an ox's portion each of grief?*
He crumpled slowly in his seat and had
his heart attack again, and I was right.

# A Diner

*Ithaca, NY, 1972*

Saturday mornings I'd take my young sons
to breakfast while my wife slept late. They liked
to spin on the counter stools, so I plunked
myself between them and slowed them down,
left, right, left, right, until our food came: juice,
milk, French toast doused by "surp," crinkled bacon.
Caption: Young father shepherding his sons.
But what if one began to weep? "Jesus,"
he snuffled, "save me; my teacher hates me."
And the other spun so fast on his stool
he spread his arms wide to keep his balance
and thus raked his plate, like a sopped discus,
into his neighbor's purse. Only a fool
would hope to be absolved, or maybe three.

# No

There may be in the air I breathe
some molecule Empedocles once took in
and let out, or maybe not.
I think it all goes utterly away
and that the future, coming fast,
of all that we remember is to be
soon forgot, even an afternoon
like this. Out for a walk after
lunch we could smell rain coming,
we could feel it through our skins,
though how, exactly, it will feel
to be drenched by today
we can't, of course, as usual, foretell:
the dog that hates thunder going
beserk, each yelp a higher rung
on a burning ladder; the turtle
on the next terrace scrunched under
an overturned fig crate; the lights
stuttering three times, then falling
mute; the lightning coming closer
with each snap, like a vast whip;
the church bells breaking thinly through
the thunder every quarter hour;
the undulant green Tiber valley roiling
full with rain and fog in billows.
A poster for an Umbrian edition
of *La Nazione* blows soggily across

the same piazza where this morning
we first saw the headline: *Grosso
Pitone Trovato Vivo Tra I Rifiuti*
(Huge Python Discovered Living in the Dump).
Then there's a fusillade
of high-pitched clatter on the roof—
tiles: hail, cloudy pellets of it
leap and sizzle at the windows.
A long rip of lightning sears
across the sky so close we both
blanch back a little from the sill
and laugh, we're so giddy
and animally alert. There must be
some way these perceptions,
each fierce, beloved flash of them,
can be kept from, in the apt phrase
of the cliche, thin air, the very air
Empedocles may or may not have breathed.

## Smart Money

We talk about—what else?—the old days.
It was time we complained about then:
"What's your poison?" the barkeep would say,
and we all knew. Now we're on the wagon,
which, these days, as then, doesn't travel far.
How did the old joke go? "Driven to drink?
It's only half a block. Why take the car?"
No way this was the road to hell—succinct,
unpaved, a scuffle of blurred dirt. We sat
like drowsy money in a bank, the mold
of interest growing on us, minus
some paltry fees, minus taxes, minus
the unexpected costs of growing old.
And then our ship came in, and we were it.

# Sentence

Bloated and mesmerized by raspberries,
the possum wobbled into the open
like a blinking child come out to the sun
from an afternoon movie, and because
time takes no time in a poem, I can hear
the guns bray and smell the spattered bowels
and fermented berries, I can hold
my hands like wafers athwart my ears,
I can feel like a fog in my nostrils
the sudden, fragrant compost, half-shit, half-
food, all memory, though I was too young
to remember much but the future: one
death, one fiesta, one sweet stench like a flag,
one possum at a time and the vast fields.

# The Dogs of Monotone at Dusk

Jockeyed by fleas and led, as we say
with lazy disdain for our senses,
by the nose, that paradigm of scouts,
they are the book that could be filled
with what they don't know. With what
they do know, you could fill a town.
People, too, coil down like water

through the spiralled streets to the piazza,
the basin of the town. The dogs
that aren't asleep or being fed
snuffle along the uric stones.
The San Francesco bells sound
8:15 and the valley,
trough of a thousand shades

of green, begins to fill like a parched well
with dusk. The sun, the color
of blood orange juice, subsides like a toy
boat in flames. Streetlights buzz on
and bats unfurl. Two (or three?) dogs,
like raddled islands, bark: the lake
of the black night is everywhere.

# Dazzle

I need some kind of talisman or charm
to protect those I love from my drear charm.

"Regret is the fruit of pity," grumbled
Genghis Khan, fingering a good luck charm.

Parkas, guns, trap-lines and ice-fishing. Who
wouldn't turn her head to surprise some charm?

He blushed. He fumbled in his lap and at
his feet. Dear God help him find his lost charm.

If it's not under pressure, it's not grace,
but only manners. Or, even worse, charm.

# Keep A-Knockin'

*I'm gonna ring your bell till I break your door,*
Little Richard rasped, and battered another
white piano out of tune and left on its keys
a roux of sweat and rouge. His lisps and yelps
and panic-driven trills were probably
a frantic dialogue between body and soul,
both of them more or less mute but for music.
Remember the little whimpering erotic

yip he lets out: *Oh! my soul.* A friend
once found himself next to Little Richard
on a plane. "I know who you are," he blurted out.
"You sure do," said Little Richard heartily,
and lowered his eyelids. *The boy always
had eyelids,* an old woman told me in Macon,
where the boy grew up. And then he said it
again: "You sure do. I'se a child of God."

# The Village Vanguard

They stop you at the bottom of the stairs.
You pay the cover and drink minimum
(no credit cards) before you can go in.
They point out tables you can't have. The air
swirls with smoke, German, Japanese and French—
this drab spot is a mecca. The night Lee
Konitz came to listen to Clark Terry
he had that good table there. You had the bench.
"The first set was three minutes short last night,"
you heard the owners scold a master once.
Why come back thirty years? Why do the bands
work so hard? How did Freud explain the bond
between grandchildren and grandparents?
They have a common enemy.

# A Citizen

That summer solstice in Alaska
I could read outdoors long past dusk, whenever
that was—the light never paled—if I could stand
the mosquitoes rippling in the night's blanched
air like veils, they were so thick and communal
of purpose. I'd not have known when dawn
came but for the bird's stark, sweet, insistent
roll call. 2:19 a.m.? OK. Because
we die, we keep records. The papers enjoyed
the plight of Anchorage Muslims: it was
Ramadan and they were forbidden food
and sex from dawn to dusk, and feeling squinched.
Dispensation made its way from a mosque
in Calgary: they could observe the sunrise
And sunset times from the Edmonton paper.
That day three Alaskans had called the place
I live *America*, a name they'd shed.
Here's what I did: I took my book outside,
God knows what it was, another frail lever
plied against the light and silence, let's say,
until the mosquitoes drove me inside,
then I stayed there until my restlessness
led me out to stretch and yawn like a cat.

## The Holiday Inn/Scope, Norfolk, Virginia, Spring, 1980

Reagan had brought his genial, low-watt
campaign, replete with Secret Servicemen,
to "our" hotel. Whose? A convention
of writers (something like a herd of cats).
"The candidate will come down soon," someone
cried out, and no elevator would budge
for anyone until he did. The public
got cordoned off by Secret Servicemen
to make a wide aisle for their man to stride.
The restaurant gleamed across the lobby.
He didn't come down and nobody moved.
Why choose between fatuousness and food?
"Dinner reservations," I cried loudly,
and, like a parade float, crossed the aisle.

# Television and Piqua, Ohio

*for Stanley Plumly*

From Piqua, Ohio—where nobody
but the librarian could tell you
how the town got its gnarl of a name,
six vowels in only nine letters, unless
"from the Indians" seems a good answer
to you—it's easy to reach Manhattan—
where "from the Indians" means something wholly

else and where Ed Sullivan and his wife
lived for years in a hotel. They ate out
every night and then took in a show,
although on Sunday nights the show was Ed's:
animal acts, Anna Moffo singing
*Caro nome*, acrobats, a boxer
and a curate rising from their comped seats

to take—and isn't "take" just the right verb?—
a bow. In Piqua you could turn a dial
and Manhattan sent you what it thought you
ought to want. Did I say it was easy
to reach Manhattan from Piqua? I should
have said it was ease itself for Manhattan
to reach Piqua; Piqua turned the dial.

"The babe that sucks the nurse to sleep," Shakespeare
called Cleopatra's asp....
                    TV also brought
us the black horse at JFK's funeral,
the perky teacher vaporized in space,
Leonard Bernstein's lectures and thirty-one
Super Bowl halftimes. We get, in fact,
more or less the same proportion of dross

to gold that untelevised life provides,
though life happens to us directly, where-
as TV is like an IV that pumps
lurid rumors into us at the right
pace to jam signals from our solitudes.
For solitude you need a farm or city,
or a book. The global village, just like

a small one or the economy, disdains
privacy, second thoughts and truculence.
And Piqua, if anyone into whose arm
the narcoleptic thrum was being oozed
would think of it....
                    And why would he or she?
Reader, gentle or not, it's up to us.
Repeat after me: Piqua, Piqua, Piqua.

## Moshe Dor, Country

*That is no country for old men...*
　　　　　　—W. B. Yeats

No, that is no country for old men,
nor for their rage about their years,
nor for the rust and squeaks of joints.
Nor their tenacities: they balk
like mules. Time nonetheless calls out
its merciless instructions.
So what country is meant for them?
Where are its peaks, its troughs,
its hamlets? What canopy of sky
shelters these old men from their faults
and fantasies they can't give up
until the ghost gives them up? And what
sea rocks them in its blue hammock,
changed to green as mercurially
as mermaids giggle? No, that is no
country for old men, but you,
who have already killed, as Jezebel
had Naboth killed, and taken
possession, as Ahab then usurped
Naboth's vineyard, think of this:
before crossing the rickety
wooden bridge you can't re-cross
the other way, dawdle a little,
think of how that is no country
for old men yet one for you and me,
our constant hunger in spite

of parables, the hunt, the hunter,
the stars, the trampled grass,
the wind slowing to silence, the hairs
on your nape moving to my breath.

# Out

Because I'm undosing myself
from nicotine, I zonk Velcro
with catnip. She's out like a light?
Like a base-stealer, not cat-quick
but tuned-out-torpid? Like a teen-
ager? Like a gay man (the non-
smoker strides coughless from the closet)?
Out out damn spot on the X-ray
of the lung? But usually out
means inward first: the recoil
before the shot. First you fall in
on yourself like a dwindling fire.
The dread you smoked to keep at bay
stays in with a sick friend. That's you.
When you're sick enough of being
sick, then you and the fire go out.

## Sad Stories Told in Bars: The Reader's Digest Version

First I was born and it was tough on Mom.
Dad felt left out. There's much I can't recall.
I seethed my way to speech and said a lot
of things: some were deemed cute. I was so small
my likely chance was growth, and so I grew.
Long days in school I filled, like a spring creek,
with boredom. Sex I discovered soon
enough, I now think. Sweet misery!

There's not enough room in a poem so curt
to get me out of adolescence, yet
I'm nearing fifty with a limp, and dread
the way the dead get stacked up like a cord
of wood. Not much of a story is it?
The life that matters not the one I've led.

# STORIES

# Growing Old

Long ago we moved to a town so small the sign on the bank said *Bank*. There was also *Gas* and a *Bar*, and the bank president's house: no sign, but a widow's walk like a howdah on its back.

The town was so snug in its valley that when Nora and I first drove over the ridge on a clear, nearly soundless day in early fall, she began to weep in huge, looping, helpless sobs, so tiny, perfect and inactive did the village seem from the rim of its bowl. Trees were about to turn, but not yet. The uncrinkled lake lay like a wide slate across the valley. I turned to her manfully and lied. I told her everything would be OK.

Trees turned and froth on the lake-waves began to glint gray. Soon the Canada geese would tilt down from the flyway onto the lake. They would outnumber the villagers at least a hundred to one, and at night, as the sky darkened and the last of the geese settled on the blackening waters after a day of foraging in the hillside fields, goose gossip rose in the grainy dusk.

These bucolic rhythms drove Nora—the way a sort of wind we never had in the valley might have driven before it waves we therefore never had—to dreams and broodings new to us both. She would wake at 3:00 a.m. with a cramp in her toe, and at 5:00 with a spider bite on one knee, and finally at 6:30 from a dream in which I and a team of surgeons had agreed she needed surgery and were trying to persuade her it would be OK. "I'm growing old," she'd snipe at me one time, and flirt at me another and pout at me yet another, and four terrible times pronounce in a dead language, "I'm growing old and you don't notice or care." We were both twenty-three.

Nora was, more and more, a handsome woman. When she sat with her legs crossed the bones in her calves were like creases in freshly pressed slacks. This tall, lantern-jawed woman seemed so achingly beautiful to me, so solid and material, that I felt evanescent, as if I could evaporate from an excess of good luck, or from the strain of being a man who deserved her lifelong company, she who was growing old and I didn't care or notice.

She sat around the house too much, I decided. We would play tennis, finding in the back of some closet rackets given to us by hopeful parents when we were gawky adolescents.

"The game will stand you in good stead long after you're too old for basketball," my father had told me with a tone in his voice like a health teacher's.

I was secretly too old for basketball then, seventeen when he told me that. A fourteen-year-old had taken me to town and back on the Longfellow playground the day before. He was so good I played the whole game in a grim, combative silence. He was all jabber. Towards the end he learned where I liked to be on the court and had started denying me those places: he got to them first. At the end I made two furiously improvised moves, playing out of a pure and undirected hatred, and they worked, and so the margin I lost by was, I told myself, respectable. In fact, I told myself, if I hadn't lost my nerve and concentration, I could have taken this kid.

"You wanna go again some other time," I said without a question mark.

"Prolly not," he said. I never saw him again.

Tennis would be my game for middle-age and my wife would be my partner.

"I look horrible in this dress," she would say, staring mournfully at her long and pretty legs. She was beginning to lose weight, of which she had never carried very much, and her bone structure was triumphant. "Shorts. I'll wear shorts."

She had a wonderful backhand. It is supposed to be the easiest stroke in tennis, because no matter how odd it looks and mirror-like it feels, it uses the fewest muscles in the most natural way. She had a mediocre forehand. Her wan serve plopped short in the service box and when she was serving and I was at the net, in doubles, our opponents would beat the ball back at me and I felt foolish and blamed her. I would edge closer to the alley because I hated to be passed on that side: if I were beaten down the middle it would more clearly be her fault as well as mine.

If we were losing I would try harder to serve harder the farther we fell behind. The harder I sprang at such serves the less frequently they went in. Nora and I would have exchanged gnarled glances by this point in the match. We would be losing and the other team graceful in victory.

"Nice try!" the man would call out as Nora netted a forehand. Or, to me, from either one of them, "That's quite a serve when it's in." Nora would be at the net, lax and long-stemmed, turning her hips back and forth though her neck stayed straight as a plumb. "Ummph," I served, just low and wildly enough to hit her in the fold in back of her right knee.

"God," I said. "I'm sorry, hon."

"Hon," she said, walking back toward me, as I had been walking toward her before something in her bearing stopped me. She said it as if it had been stuck between her teeth. "Hon." There was only a tiny pause. "Hon, you son-of-a-bitch, you pun, you phoney." I've always marveled at "you pun," and not only for the rhyme. I tell myself that it makes the whole episode typical, remarkable, true, and less likely actually to have happened.

She grew older, as she feared, and grew more beautiful and less haughty. I remember her after that match (4-6, 0-6) standing with her back to the mirror, looking over one shoulder and then the other at the bruise purpling the back of her knee, as if it might be a liver spot.

I had money I hadn't dreamed of when I first dawned over the ridge with Nora. I imagined spreading it like a winning hand of cards on the realtor's desk. "I understand the bank president's house is for sale." I had a fever and money.

"Some people think the widow's walk is unsightly," he said. I wrote him a huge check.

Nora's house—our old house—is across the street. There's little traffic and sometimes I can hear her singing. I sit on the third floor, with the widow's walk above me and the rest of my too big house below me, and with the windows open, and I read, staring out over the lake now and then. Her singing sounds like conversations you hear sometimes in the dim background when you make a long distance call. What you hear is not words or argument, but rhythm, inflection, pacing, tone of voice, the voice itself but nothing that it says.

# Nessun Dorma

I'd agreed to take Clara's cat from Iowa City to Boulder, and there's a story in that, all by itself, but I won't tell it; I'll just scurry along with this one.

Clara brought me the cat scrunched and wretched in a catbox, but silent. I loaded my old VW to the gunnels and put the catbox in last, atop a box of books and papers and right behind me so it didn't block my view in the mirror. Then I turned the key in the ignition and pulled out of the driveway and the cat began to yowl—a steady, grating, keening sound. I'd figured the drive for eighteen hours. I sure would hate to listen to eighteen hours of this, I thought, and the cat yowled as faithfully as a pulse or a schoolroom clock for every hour we were in the car together.

Twice in the first hundred miles I stopped and tried to improvise a silence.

Once I took the cat out of her box so she could roam around the car, and here's what went wrong. The cat skulked under my seat and yowled metronomically, and whenever I moved my right foot from the accelerator to the brake or vice-versa, she surged out from her lair and slashed at my ankles. I tried to ignore her and she yowled. I cursed her and she clawed her way up the back of the driver's seat and wrapped herself around the back of my neck, like a stole, and she yowled, so I stopped at a gas station where she hissed through the window at a torpid dog while I put her back in her box, from which she continued to yowl.

I drove a few more miles and then I pulled over again and moved some stuff around so I could put the catbox in the well behind the driver's seat. I opened every window and turned the radio up full blast and set out west again. The cat's constant yowls rose above the din the way Birgit Nilsson's voice could float like reflected moonlight on the whole ocean of the chorus in a crowd scene, in *Turandot*, for example. So I hummed and she yowled and we drove through the heat across the plains into the beckoning dust. If humming isn't enough, I thought, I'll sing.

People who grew up somewhere else love to complain about the long drive across Nebraska. A friend used to tell about a family hegira across the scorched and treeless wastes in the full furnace of mid-July, everyone snarky from the heat and looking for a tree under which to eat their wilting and spoiling sandwiches. They spy a fluffy splinter on the horizon. A tree! They slog and slog. Finally they arrive. They burst out of the car, spread a blanket, distribute the picnic goodies. Just as my friend is about to take a first bite from his sandwich the wind—where had it been all morning?—burgeons from the west and blows the turkey slice like a limp frisbee clean out of his sandwich, so that he chomps down on two slices of bread and a buffer of rancid mayonnaise.

It's not like that. The brown and greens come in a couple dozen varieties each. From the straight interstate you can watch the sine-curved aisles of cottonwoods escort the river along its meanders. I grew up on the plains but they were beautiful long before I was born. I could drive across Nebraska a week and be happy, but not with the cat going off and on like an alarm, so I drove as fiercely as she squalled.

So when I got twelve hours out (and six to go) I pulled into a motel the AAA book had told me would take pets. I'd called ahead to make sure. I asked again at the desk and paid in advance so I could hit the road early. I took an overnight bag out of the trunk and then opened the car and took out the catbox and the plastic tray of cat litter—this cat was either constipated or on strike, I'd discovered at a series of rest stops—and into our room we went. I shut the door and loosed the cat. She streaked under the bed, slung nearly as low to the carpet as a snake, her four elbows, or whatever you call them on a cat, poking up above her slinking body, and disappeared under the bedspread. Thunk! It was a pedestal bed. She ricocheted back out, wild now, and sped around the room like a pinball.

So I stalked her and caught her and held her. It was like holding a furred plank. She started to yowl but twice as fast as before. "Oh God," I wondered, "can a cat hyperventilate?" I didn't know what else to do so I got into bed and lifted the covers. She dove in, squirmed down to my feet and quivered there, silent now, and bit my feet whenever I moved them.

Two hours of not sleeping like that were enough, so I put the cat back in the box, from which it began to yowl, and hit the road.

The plot of *Turandot* is no more likely than this shaggy cat story. Turandot is an Ice Princess, see, but the man who can answer three riddles posed by her father—and these are trick questions, mind you—can marry her. Contestants who fail die. They have twenty-four hours. Calif is yet another burly but loveable tenor who's a fool for love, so he signs on. Given the stakes and the time limit, contestant forego their sleep routines. The populace loves this national gossip—isn't that what royal families are for?—and they're up all night, too. Nobody sleeps, which is how you might translate the unofficial title of Calif's boffo aria, *nessun dorma*. You can tell right away that the contestants who scour the country-side for answers, as if love and death were an Easter egg hunt, are dead meat, as they say in the Mafia movies. You have to look for the answers into your very heart, that engine room, that attic, that bus station at 4:00 a.m., that rust-pocked and over-heating VW slowly toiling up from the plains to the high plains to the eastern face of the Rockies.

But I'm getting ahead of myself. Of course that's easy to do when you're dealing with these creaky and obvious plots. Imagine having to solve problems devised by a woman's father just to love her. Imagine that love is one door and death another, just like that. And imagine that you're made so vivid and alert by all this foolery that you step forward and sing about it, pouring out the very heart into which you've just now remembered to look. It's one thing to sing and another to believe what you're singing.

Real life is a long drive. The odometer slowly erodes the miles from Iowa City to Boulder, the cat yowls, you stop for gas, you stop to pee. You don't stand beside a coolerful of tepid pop in a Sunoco station's grease bay in Silt, Nebraska, and sing that your urine is like a warm and mighty river. You do your business and then you get back in the car and do that business, too, and eventually you're home.

When I got in, finally, I was of course earlier than I'd predicted to the tenant, who had agreed to be out of my house by noon that day, and he was in the shower. I let the cat out of her box and it was as if she'd never been gone. She started marauding for crickets in the scruffy, meadowy yard, and she had in her throat that hypnotized, rapine whir I'd not heard for a year. She leapt and stalked. I made myself a mug of coffee and wandered idly around my house. I drummed my fingers on a window casement and straightened a chair to my liking. Through the kitchen window I could see the cat plying her trade. In a drawer in the sideboard I found a cache of condoms among the candles for the dinner table, and in the refrigerator sweet juices: pineapple and guava. Soon it would all be mine again, though. I could almost feel the deliberate spin of the earth under my feet, through the floor and foundation of the house, the world seemed so blessedly regular.

At last my tenant was ready and pointed toward the door.

"Probably I should tell you there was a break-in." No condoms stolen, I hope, I found myself thinking while I stood waiting to hear the rest. Where does the mind come up with its amusements? "They must have gone out the back door as I came in the front."

"What'd they get?" I asked casually.

"Some roast beef. Some bread. I found crumbs leading from the kitchen to the back door. I guess they were hungry."

"That's all?"

"That's all."

He returned his set of keys and we shook hands and he left.

It was time for a shower for me, and then I closed the shades against the midday sun and just before I hit the sack, as tired as I ever remember being, I called Clara.

"How did she take the trip?"

"She yowled all the way."

"Oh God, I was afraid of that."

There must have been a little more patter, but the next thing I can remember saying is, "I'm exhausted; I've got to sleep." A slight pause. "Listen . . . Thrive and prosper in New York."

"Thanks. I'm planning on it." Slight pause. "And listen . . . Don't worry. She'll be alright."

# Blue Streak

Now this would be an outing. On Saturday morning across America sad weekend dads might be herding their children to Mcdonald's, but Ron had Jason and Mark dressed up, prim and scrunched and slithery at once, and they were off to Boston.

The train ride itself would be an adventure.

"You'll have them every other weekend," Sam, his twice-divorced lawyer had said, "and two months in the summer. I'd sign it and stay out of court. Believe me."

"That's great," Ron had said, because maybe it was. "They'll have two homes."

"Where the friends are, where the school is, where they walk home from a pal's and hear a dog growl and know its name and who owns it, that's home, you know what I mean? You're an adventure, and kids hate adventure. They want the same food, the same rules, the same arguments about how much they can watch TV. They want re-runs. You want my advice?"

Ron didn't.

"Get a pet and make them feed it. Give them chores. One month in the summer, send them to camp. Kids love routines. Ex-wives love routines. They love to win the daily custody and cook for the kids and bitch about it and put the band-aids on and joke about it, perky and deserted and brave. And it wins the kids. And why not? For love you gotta be there."

"Jesus," thought Ron.

"Re-runs?" Ron asked.

"Yeah," said Sam. "You know. Ricky the Spic tells what's-her-name, Blue Streak, The Redhead, not to spend any money and he goes off to work and then he comes home and she's got a new vacuum cleaner and all hilarious hell breaks loose: the machine pukes dirt and they screech at other but everyone's in character and the audience licks it up.

It's familiar. Family life is repetition."

"Jesus," thought Ron; Ellen, his soon-to-be-ex-wife, was half-*chicana*.

"Get a pet," said Sam. "Get a cat. Until they invent the shitless dog, you live in an apartment, you need a cat."

"Sam," Ron began . . .

"Lucy!" Sam cried.

But the train trip itself would be an adventure. An hour to Boston, then the Science Museum—good for kids—and on to Fenway Park, where a hot dog was not junk food but nearly a sacrament.

Sam was just rancid with anger, and adventure's good name undefiled.

Ron and Jason and Mark—"Why don't you ever say Mark and Jason?" Mark had started to ask—stood on the platform like longtime commuters and bowed slightly from the waist and twisted their trunks slightly and peered up the track to see if this courtliness had made the train more visible. And maybe it had, for here came the train.

Mark would have the window on the trip in and Jason on the trip home, when, as he pointed out, it might be dark, if the game went into extra innings, for example, and so Mark had clearly won the day in advance and why would Mark bother to grow up when he get whatever he wanted by acting the baby, the favorite, the kissass. . .

"No," said Ron, quite sharply, "none of this. Today's an adventure."

So Jason piped down and sat in the middle to make a show of craning around and over Mark to see the outside world recede, and Ron sat on the aisle, as if to be a buffer between his unruly and heartbreaking children and the other passengers, and crossed his legs and tried not to look or even to be morose.

The train started off with a sort of cough or stammer, but enough of a convulsion to unbalance anyone still in the aisle, and the woman next to Ron—about sixty, wearing a too dressy and too often dry cleaned white rayon sheath and an orange scarf with blues whales on it and a tatty straw hat with blurry artificial flowers—lurched toward Ron, the back of her thigh hitting the sole of his left shoe where it was crossed over his right leg and sticking, he realized, slightly but culpably into the aisle.

"I see," she said, whirling on him. "You're young, you can do whatever you like with your foot." She was ablaze, this frowsy Carmen, and staring at the sooty outline of a shoe sole on her dress. "You're an oaf, you do what you want, you take your little oaflets with you and teach them your smutty tricks, you break wind, you stare, you swallow, you don't even"—and by now she was out of breath and took on a sob's worth—"apologize. Look at this," she was yelling now and pointing to her smirched haunch, and jutting it an inch or two toward him for emphasis, "look at this." And now her face began to crumple, though her voice rose steadily. "You want the streets and the aisles of the train and the malls and the good chairs in the library. Curse you, sir," she wailed and turned and started away, "and everyone you ever care for."

He had been pinned to his seat by all this, carefully not looking at Mark or Jason, but now that she was done he called out in a clear voice, "Good God Ma'am, I'm terribly sorry."

"Don't swear at me," she cackled, and surged ahead.

And then he rose from his seat and followed her full speed, with long, loping paces, and caught her just as she reached the end of the car. She could hear him coming, he could see from a vast flinch of her small shoulders, and she spun around again and faced him, tears coursing down her cheeks, and spread her arms, and looked a little over his right shoulder and demanded of her onlookers, the world and Ron, "What are you going to do now, hit me?"

# Blues 52

The bassist, the boy, the bambino, had broken a string. The last set the last night of a week-long gig. So he stands there with that grin slant on his face like someone ran by at full speed and slapped it on his mouth and it stuck. His big number is next: he goes four or five minutes in the middle. I get to lay out; he gets to shine. You run a band, you're managing calories.

I don't know what they mean by a "sheepish" grin. You seen a sheep show more than half-a-blade-of-grass's worth of emotion? I mean on its face? They panic, they run. They cool, they eat. Sheep life is low on subtlety, know what I mean?

It's people like the bambino got sheepish grins. So what I do is, I take the microphone and I announce the bambino gonna work the Fender 'cause he broke a string on his acoustic bass. I don't ask him, I tell everybody else. So we run through the melody once and bend it a little twice and then he's on. Eighteen years old, the bambino.

And he's very happy up there, big grin, rocking his hips the tiniest bit, sticking a little (twanggg) vibrato on the end of his phrases, you know, Tennessee or something.

I'm happy, too. I have to lean on the bartender a little for the vodka & OJ he promised me between sets, but then I get to sit back and sip and watch the bambino ply that Fender.

Course I came up with Art Blakey, the one-man Harvard University of jazz, and I was a sprout when he hired me, right after Lee Morgan took his degree and split. Super-boy with his lip of steel, but I didn't know plenty and Blakey had plenty to teach. So I hire the whiz kids myself. Take Benny, my piano man. Twenty-five maybe? Just before he died, Art says to me, "That kid can play." Benny looks like the president of the chess club up there, flopping around in those check suits he likes, loose shoulders that boy's got and feet like aircraft carriers. But he can hear the structure of a song as fast as anyone.

"These kids keep me young," Art used to tell the folks, and he stayed so young he up and died. Seventy-one.

Now the bambino's done so I wander back to the stand and we take that one out. One more. Long week. One more. Time to say a few words to the folks.

So I tell them how they've been a great crowd, even for New York where the crowds are notoriously tough. It doesn't hurt to congratulate an audience, even when they deserve it. How I came east to record but first for some practice and to play this gig, how I bust my motherfucking lip, how I missed the first night of the gig, how it all worked out because once it's the past it's only the path you took to get to the present.

I love to do the patter because somewhere along the ramble of it I always have a clear picture of myself as a kid with a horn standing around waiting to go on, stiff as a statue, not one ounce of relaxation or confidence anywhere in that scrawny body. The name of the statue is Terror. The longer I'm up there now charming and thanking every-one the longer the statue's got before he has to thaw those baby muscles and go out there and play over his head just to keep shame off his case.

Then I introduce every one in the band again, lots of lauds and thanks. And I do love those kids. I do the drums and the sax and I tell everyone the bambino's age, and then I swirl around, Mr. Melodrama, and lean across the back of the piano and grin at Benny, who's sitting there all attentive and respectful, and there's a yellow spot on me and I get my face in the true center of it. I don't ever look away from Benny.

"And I'm fifty-two," I say. "Now this gentleman here is about the reverse of that, twenty-five, and he comes to me with diplomas and letters of recommendations and the praise of the great. Art told me the gentleman could play and Art was right, of course. Well, shee-it, I said, I better listen up 'cause maybe I can hire me a genius."

You know how you hold a stage grin long enough you start to look like a man died in the middle of a smile? I was like that and Benny had his I'm Paying Close Attention look on for my whole monologue, but underneath it, peeping around the sides, I could see his What He's Doing To Me Now look. So I went for a long pause and then I tripled it. Benny's squirming without moving a muscle. Maybe I was a little hard on him but shit, fifty-two. You're his age, you think you're paying dues fast as you can breathe, and one day you be done. All you're doing is waiting in line for the hard part.

So finally I've held the pause long enough twice and I say, "And probably I have hired me a genius," and I mean it.

Then we run an encore. You know how the place is laid out: you got to go upstairs to get to the dressing rooms. So at the end I've got the bell mute in, and the drink-stingy management dims the room lights, and I walk off the stage still doodling a little, quite slow, and to the bottom of the stairs, and then halfway up there's that bend in the stairs, and all the time I'm playing a little more softly, but so they can still hear me. Shades of Jimmy Fucking Durante. What I like is how I can hold them off: they're ready to put their hands together, but I got a few little blue doodles left for them, and so they can't, not yet.

# Doc Holliday's Grave

Three of us trudged up a winding street about a car-and-a-half wide, and where the street gave out a scruffy path continued, about a shoe-and-a-half wide, and it wound up and up. It was ten a.m., maybe, but the ground at 8,500 feet above sea level was already tenderfoot hot. Across the valley sheer cliffs rose, probably four miles away, but through the Colorado air you could see not a smudge of evergreens but individual trees, no two alike, Ponderosa pines. You ever see a seedling for a Ponderosa pine? It's perfectly adapted to live high and dry. The inch or two of it that will be above ground looks like the tip of a new branch, symmetrical and tentative. The taproot's four times longer.

We slogged ten minutes on that path, it steeper by the minute and we shallower of breath, and then we were on a small plateau cantilevered out from the steep mountain-side we'd been climbing. Here was where Glenwood Springs, Colorado, kept its early dead, foremost among them Doc Holliday, the famous gunman, a dentist from Baltimore who'd died in his sleep.

From the cemetery you could stare across to the answering cliffs on the other side and until you thought to lower your gaze you'd not see the valley with its coiled, glittering river and spatters of irrigated green where the living clumped and a few of them played golf. As long as you didn't drop your glance you were in the parched, mineral west, a speck on a mountain with less purchase there than a settlement of lichen. The dead are only here by courtesy of the mountain, you could think, a little dreamily, catching your breath, and so are their heirs and assigns down the slope.

"Let's meet for breakfast and then go see Doc Holliday's grave," one of us had said the night before, and here we were.

French toast in The Rough Rider Room, for the hotel had once been Teddy Roosevelt's vacation White House, as the press today would call it.

Doc, Teddy. "Don't call me Mr. President. This is America—no titles here." Doc, Teddy and Aunt Jemima, she of the kerchief and syrup, served here in tiny plastic tubs from which the foil lids had to be carefully peeled back lest there be a sticky mishap.

At the next table a father said carefully to his daughter, "Here, honey, let me do that for you."

"No," she said, "I wanna."

"Joanna," he said, and I could feel him working to be reasonable, "you've got your party dress on."

"No," she shrilled, and jerked away as the lid tore loose and the blobs of syrup flew.

"Joanna, damn it," he began, and then lowered his voice, and try as I might I couldn't hear the rest.

Doc Holliday, I was thinking, and Count Basie, and Duke Ellington.

Paul was botanizing. The higher the altitude the more plant names he knew. There was Wild Hyacinth (sometimes Cluster-lily, sometimes Bluedicks, sometimes confused with Nodding Onion): "You don't often see it this high." I wasn't sure if he meant the plant grew usually closer to the ground or seldom at this altitude. There was Bitterbrush (sometimes Brittlebrush): paled, yellow rose-shaped flowers, as I remember them, tiny and fragrant. So the name must come from their taste, or the taste of the leaves, or some taste you have already in your mouth, such as the difference between the names of things and things themselves, that you notice while staring at the beautiful, paled, yellow rose-shaped flowers.

Of course Paul liked to hold forth. Paul was too classy for a tattoo, but if he'd had one, stencilled into his tongue by someone who hated him, perhaps, it would read BORN TO KNOW STUFF.

What was hard to figure about Paul was Tam. Paul had, as well as all that ready knowledge, the attributes of class, but they were undermined by restlessness, a kind of truancy: wherever Paul was he seemed already bored by it and poised for flight.

Tam had class itself. She didn't say everything she knew, she didn't look over your shoulder at parties to see who else was in the room, she lowered her eyes when praised and then raised them back to look frankly into your pleased face.

What was she doing with Paul, who was talking about outlaws now?

"... the protection of property. That's why Wells Fargo had its own security force. In Puccini's opera *La Fanciulla del West*, set in the Sierra Nevadas during the gold rush..."

Paul wouldn't require an assistant in order to turn himself into a 24-hour FM station. I imagined him lying on his back, with a transmission tower rising from his chest like a stake from a vampire.

We stayed half an hour more. Mostly I stared out over the valley wondering what sorts of lives were lived there, and once or twice I stared at Tam, when she didn't know I was looking, and wondered what sort of life she was living.

Then it was time to go back down. Tam started down first and I fell in behind her. Then Paul tried to come around on the path, which was far too narrow for such a maneuver, and so he jostled me and I nearly fell.

I'd been watching Tam's pert little ass sway back and forth as she picked her way down the path, and if I'd been asked what frame of mind was mine just before Paul bumped me, I'd have called it lazy or day-dreamy, nearly pre-verbal.

But the words were suddenly swarming, and I swung myself around to square off with Paul and loosed them.

"You know, pal, you're more than a little bit the outlaw yourself, self-absorbed and wholly, I mean wholly, unreliable to others. It wouldn't be hard to imagine you pulling a man's tooth one minute and then shooting him in the jaw the next. Damn you, Paul..."

Paul was stunned. "I'm sorry I ran into you, man," he blurted out, and shifted his weight, nearly falling forward as he did, and so he reached out his arm to put a hand against my chest to stop himself from pitching over.

So I pretended to misinterpret that move and I balled my fist and hit him. He flung his cupped hands at his face, as if to keep the pain in, but before they got there he spat and I could see part of a tooth fly out.

"Shit," he said, "you broke my tooth."

"Jesus," said Tam. She had her hands on her hips. "What a pair of first class louts." She turned and started back downhill.

Paul and I had to find the local hospital and then sit a few minutes in the foyer of the emergency room, a silent pair of first class louts, until somebody came out to pay attention to his tooth while I explained to the woman in admissions, I think they called it, how I would pay for whatever attentions Paul required. All this took an hour and a half and by the time we were back to the hotel Tam was checked out and gone.

She and Paul are no longer together, of course, and I never see her. The concert trail being what it is, Paul's path and mine cross now and again. Our careers still take us to lots of places like Glenwood Springs, but we're both working more or less steadily.

If he sees me coming through a crowd at a party to greet him, he'll start rubbing his chin and begin to grin a little ruefully. "I can predict the emotional weather with this tooth," he'll be saying by the time I'm at hand-shake's length, "and here's the man I have to thank for it." The person he's been talking to, often an attractive young woman, will be composing that about-to-hear-a-story look on her face.

"Good to see you, Paul," I'll say, and he'll turn a little bit toward me to include me in the group, and he'll grin a little harder, and then he'll tell the story, a little differently each time, though he never fails to mention, somewhere along the line, that Doc Holliday died in his sleep.

One Close Escape after Another

for Coleman Barks

We had scheduled Bill Shakespeare for a poetry reading on 16 April, but then we discovered that was his birthday and he was already slated to read at Avon College, whose Director of Creative Writing explained that they had sent out their publicity, they knew how to take care of business even if we didn't, they wouldn't budge and the conflict in dates was our problem. He spoke in suave paragraphs with audible semi-colons. In fact we had sent out some publicity of our own-- notes pinned to swans, clouds shaped like whales, and a press release (<u>Dormant Volcano Still Inert</u>)--, but little did that fact matter to the impressario at Avon. There were pauses during our phone conversation when I'm sure he was adjusting his tie.

So what to do next? I wrote two press releases (<u>Dreams Perturb Sleepers</u> and <u>Shy Children Surround Abandoned Car</u>) and went home, troubled. The whole future of the Spring Arts Festival was at stake and the "we" I began this anecdote with had dwindled to "me," the wet torch of Western Civilization shaky in my petulant and exhausted hand, and me an assistant professor.

The next long livid day I knocked out three press releases still thought by me, and not only by me, to be the best I've ever done.

I was in a white heat. It would be immodest for me to say I'd written Cancer Caused by Power: it seemed to dictate itself.

I was a little dazed and drew myself exactingly back to my own life by writing Melancholy Travelers Trudge Home. I sweated over every syllable of that release, but can't remember one of them. It was like a lost weekend.

Next I needed a transcendant calm and wrote Tasteless Space People Loathe Mozart, with its shimmer of dimmed light.

When I woke it was near midnight. In a short piece like this it would be efficient to say it was midnight, but I cannot tell a lie, except for artistic purposes. Anyhow, it was getting damn near the 16th, the Arts Festival would be beginning soon, and I picked up the phone. Soon the sun would rise on the 16th and it wouldn't stop, it would go on, noon, afternoon, and then an audience sifting into the library auditorium, Shakespeare telling obscene theater anecdotes in the green room at Avon College and nobody on stage here, the sun long gone, the audience fitful and shifting, and the phone in my crimped hand emitting a mechanical noise it is too late and I am too tired to describe....

# ESSAYS

# The Poetry I Want

Margaret Mead notes that "primitive" societies develop personalities the way some people do: by suppressing psychic white noise. That's why such a life seems "simple." But the cost isn't invisible—it's only hidden.

A heterodox ("advanced") society tends not to suppress anything: quite literally it will blow your mind: good if your mind is a logjam or a penis, bad if it's electronic equipment or brain cells. Also, all noises seem alike. "Home" sounds like "Dallas," and "me" like "what is possible for me."

The poetry I want was raised somewhere else, like a feral child. You can't tell it how society works: it has no vocabulary. It has to develop, rather than to curse the inheritance of, self-consciousness. It can learn from anything because it belongs to nobody, nothing, no model of society. It will be forced to choose its allegiances: an act, finally, of imagination. Logic helps but you have to tell it what to do.

This poetry will ask, "Where am I going to ground all this energy?" In words, in the earth. I'll try to write such poems, because I want to read them. But it doesn't matter where they're found.

# On Reviewing

The life of American poetry is too often obscured by such essentially sociological distractions as grants, anthologies, most reviews, teaching jobs, etc. All of these enterprises contribute to the literary climate, to be sure, but usually in the ways that matter least; too, these are enterprises that have traditionally proven equally distracting to writers whether they are well or poorly administered. The envy and competitiveness these distractions encourage are more often fed than opposed by local poetry scenes and by most small magazines and little presses. In the midst of such distractions, one way to care for your share of the literary climate is to sit down with some poems, read them as intelligently and passionately as they and your own limits as a reader will allow, and to describe accurately to yourself your affections for and distrusts of those poems.

To do this in public is to write a review.

It doesn't matter, except perhaps to the poet's ego, whether a review of his or her book be "positive" or "negative": it matters that the review be intelligent. There is too much automatic praise in our reviewing—as readers and writers we ought to take ourselves seriously enough to demand the best from ourselves, and from others—and so it may be that in a sociological and therefore finally trivial way "negative" reviews are more needed, to redress a balance that won't exist tomorrow anymore than it did yesterday.

Like any passionate reader or writer of poems, I live in the hope of great poems. I want to read poems that purify the language I love without simplifying experience, that attack my pieties, that open my sense of what it feels like to be alive, that frighten and console me utterly. I expect that these yet unwritten great poems will be a kind of spiritual food, as the great poems I already know have been for me. Except to the tender and sometimes vicious egos of poets, it doesn't matter who will write them. But it matters that we have them. I can predict nothing of them, except that they will be written in solitude. And yet into that solitude the poet will carry whatever he or she knows of the language that has been loved and used by so many before, and the good wishes of readers and writers generous enough to offer them. He or she will be working in a small space—two lungs full of air, a small plot of ground. Anything we can do to make the air clean, to make the tilth of the soil healthy, is a contribution.

So why review? I do it because I have used (in the sense that one would "use" a library or the examples of a teacher) the literary climate and I want to contribute to it. Yes, I also do it because I love debate, and because I like my opinions in print. But mostly I do it because I want someone to leave his or her solitude and re-enter the shared literary climate with a great poem for which I hope I will have the sense to be immediately and needfully greedy.

# Two Takes on Richard Hugo

Late summer in Boulder, 1975, and Richard Hugo was arriving to begin a year as a visiting professor. I drove down to town from my canyon house to meet him at Reg Saner's place, and we sat outside and talked.

Hugo is an anecdotalist: his conversation has long, sure arcs, and a steady bass line. He loves Dixieland and swing, with their utilitarian structures. The melody is stated (ABA one time through), improvisations follow, and then everyone gathers to the melody and rides out. He talks like this. It's tempting to make an easy analogy to ways he writes, but one needs to remember that he also loves Mozart, whose structures are likewise solid (the sonata form is ABA, after a fashion), but whose spendthrift melodic invention is germane to Hugo, too.

He told a story that night about a cannibal in Glacier National Park. Something wild and inexplicable had driven a poor bastard to eat someone in the Park.

I knew and loved Hugo's poems enough to see the appeal the story held for him. The cannibal had degraded himself in secret; indeed, his isolation and degradation were linked. He'd crossed a line and couldn't come back. He only ate one human, but he'd be a cannibal forever, and it's as if, retroactively, he had always been a cannibal, as if by eating someone he'd finally confronted his destiny.

The cannibal got in his car and drove west, picking up a hitchhiker now and then. In California he got stopped by the Highway Patrol for a routine check—tire-tread, or emission control. He pulled a fingerbone from one pocket and confessed fervently, having found in the cop and a stunned hitch-hiker a chance to tell his story and also the misunderstanding audience he needed and felt he deserved.

Hugo rounded off his story: "Can you imagine what to say to this cannibal if you were the psychiatrist appointed to interview him first?" Reg Saner is mercurially quick, and had an answer. "First off, I'd tell him that it's wrong to eat people." We all rumbled, laughing. Saner's house is at the very base of the Flatirons, and it was freshly dark. He had provided sweaters for his guests.

Boulder is only a boutique at the base of the Rockies, and the thick, mineral black of the mountains and the sharp dark of the mile-high air combined to remind us how the west could toss its huge shoulders and shrug off everything human. In 1975 I was a recent arrival from the east, and it would be years before I understood how much western space and geology meant to what Saner and Hugo said that night.

∽

Hugo's interest is in how human beings get along, more frequently how they don't get along, and in what parallels can be made between the metaphors of the integrated psyche and the integrated community . . . [His] second book is called Good Luck in Cracked Italian. It turns out that when Hugo goes around Italy he has an incredible genius for finding disused towns that look like what he fears the state of his soul might be. And that Hugo going around Italy and Hugo going around Montana are incredibly alike, despite the fact that there's a little more age on the artifacts in Italy.

I'll read you just one poem from Good Luck in Cracked Italian. It's the "Castel Sant' Angelo," the role of which as a prison has been made famous by Puccini's opera, Tosca, which is referred to in the poem. At the end of the opera the heroine leaps off the battlement to her death.

> We order coffee made with a machine
> that gleams the name of some firm in Milan.
> Had Tosca jumped from where they claim,
> she would have splatted by that taxi in the street.

∽

> Cruelty is what a land endures before
> it's clean. Years of torture here
> fan out from us, brown miles of monument
> and dome, pigeons rising pink in haze
> and broken women scattered on the stream.
> We stand on stone and holy violence
> of men, and even late in afternoon,

> Rome seen from a parapet is always
> dawn.

Dawn is the time when Gloria Tosca makes her famous leap, which is why it's dawn at the end of the poem... Hugo has a very high number of poems about places used for jails, as dungeons, and for the administration of torture in his tour of Italy. He has a poem about people passing over the Bridge of Sighs in Venice, who are about to be incarcerated, and in almost every city he went to a jail...

One of the things that's going on is that Hugo has an ability to see beneath the monuments, the centuries of blood and violence, the "holy violence of men," as the poems say, that built the society which we, from the New World, admire so much when we go there because it has all this age and grace and glamorous history. Hugo saw instantly how much violence and what kinds of violence it had cost and went to the places that would remind him of it...

One of the things that happened on that trip to Italy, I'm sure of it, is that Hugo finds in Italy a characteristic, an idiomatic European form of the kinds of loneliness and fascination with violence and sense of isolation and depravity that he had in Montana. And he says, "No, this is not something that I have because I'm strange and warped. This is something that humans have. This is part of the radical equality of human souls..."

And so Hugo comes back from Italy a more confident poet, a far less regional poet, and a poet willing more and more to speak in the first person plural—to make the kind of connection between the body politic, the community and the integrated psyche that he had always intuitively sensed was going to be a helpful key to him in integrating (if it was ever going to be possible) that psyche.

# A Night at the White House

*On Thursday, January 3rd, 1980, Mrs. Carter hosted 100 American poets for what the next morning's Washington Post called "one of the most enjoyable White House parties in recent memory."*

The last time American poets were invited to the White House in numbers, it was for Robert Frost's 80th birthday. There was a reading at the Library of Congress, and just as the poets were about to board buses for the White House the Cuban missile crisis grew so tense the party was called off.

Why now? It seems a backer of *Poetry* magazine in Chicago made a friendly complaint to Sen. Percy that the White House was always bringing in musicians, dancers, and other performing artists, but no tribute had been paid or enjoyment got from poets. Could this be remedied? Mrs. Carter and Mrs. Mondale were approached. Yes indeed. The open date on the calendar was January 3rd, and could the editors of *Poetry* submit a preliminary guest list? Yes indeed. Things were whipped together with speedy insouciance, in the manner of Julia Child.

By the mathematics of negative capability, perhaps, or at least by the protocol of capitol party-giving, the guest list for hosting 100 poets was 500. I recognized among the supernumeraries friends of the arts (Daniel Boorstin, Library of Congress), friends of poetry (critic Helen Vendler; Peter Stitt, poetry reviewer for *Georgia Review*), cellar-masters of the national arts vineyard (Nancy Hanks and Livingston Biddle, past and current chairman, respectively, of the NEA), the rich and glamorous (Rod McKuen, rhymester), and a number of Illinois luminaries (including Anthony and Barbara Angelo, backers of *Poetry* magazine and of President Carter's Illinois campaign efforts).

There were some serious omissions from the guest list (a few distinguished older poets were sacrificed so that I and fellow younger poets could go). Very few who were invited didn't come: Odysseus Elytis, this year's Nobel Laureate, wasn't there, nor Robert Penn Warren. William Meredith, currently Poetry Consultant to the Library of Congress, was in Bulgaria for the State Department's program of artistic exchange. Muriel Rukeyser was too ill to come. Etc.

The poets had been invited each to bring a guest, and those who could afford two plane fares did.

The party was schedule for 4 – 6 p.m. The twenty-one poets who read—three in each of seven rooms, scheduled for five minutes (and thereby held to ten) each—were to arrive at 3:30, the rest of the poets at 4:00. I accompanied a nervous pal who had been tapped to read and so was early. There had been a Marine Cops string quartet playing middle Haydn and early Mozart when we were ushered in. In by the back lawn, out by the front door. People were singing and dancing, kissing (a busman's holiday, if you think of poetry as kiss-and-tell).

The crowd waiting to pass through the southwest gate of the White House was chatty, spiffy and happy. It had been a long time since poets either felt welcome at the White House or as if they wanted to go there. Volleys of greetings flew, interrupted at fifteen-minute intervals by the White House's starling-scattering system, loud electronic bleats that issued eerily from the vast back lawn.

Who was in line? Gwendolyn Brooks, James Atlas, A. R. Ammons, Linda Pastan, Jonathon Williams, Marvin Bell, David Wilk (literature program director at the NEA), Phil Levine, Stanley Kunitz, and isn't that Senator Percy's car (license: Illinois 67)? Yes indeed.

Readings were from 4:15 – 4:45. I chose the program of Phil Levine, Maxine Kumin and Sterling Brown, contemporary of Jean Toomer and Langston Hughes. To say that a very distinguished man of 93 was having "the time of his life" is presumptuous, except when he says it himself, as Sterling Brown did. Brandishing his Phi Beta Kappa key like a priest waving a cross at a vampire, he warded off the "deep, symbolic, difficult poets." He brandished quotes: "I feel like a bartender among angels."

Maxine Kumin read three poems from her recent *The Retrieval System*. Phil Levine began by noting that Whitman had advised American poets to go among their mute and simple countrymen: "And I have," he went on; "I've taught in colleges all my adult life."

Next the seven schismatic rooms convened in the East Room, where Mrs. Carter addressed everyone briefly, paid homage to the late Elizabeth Bishop, and then joined Mrs. Mondale and the President in a reception line in the long hall, like the waist of an hourglass, between the East Room and the bar in the West Room. This was the first time the guests were all in one place, and cries of recognition swarmed in the formal air. And hour and a half of intense socializing followed. As the *Washington Post* had it, "the crowd was made up largely of people who knew and liked one another, and the congeniality was ... thick." There were mini-portions of quiche and pizza, cheeses, and carafes of wine which one palate, all too attuned to the compromise between adventure and professional salary, identified instantly as Robert Mondavi White Table Wine.

The mood was as bubbly, generous and cheerful as I've seen it be at any literary gathering. In the China Room, where the place settings in use under various presidencies are displayed in lit wall-cabinets, I sat with Richard Hugo, Sandra McPherson and Henry Carlisle, Louis Simpson, Donald Hall, W. D. Snodgrass, Howard Moss (who, in a role secondary to his life as a poet, as poetry editor of *The New Yorker*, will read all too many verse-versions of how the day went).

    I stood at one time with seven poets about my age, all of whom had published some part of their best early work in a magazine I was (when we were all even brasher and younger) editing. It was the first time we had all stood physically together, and the White House had done it. Fancy meeting you here!

    Later, I stood with a poet whose work I love, and who is dying, thinned in body and voice both. Throat cancer. Not a rasped word of it, but a sandpapered and sentimental hello.

    Visible, audibly, the body of work is replacing the body of the poet.

The best comment was made by the novelist John Dranow, surveying the well-dressed and well-behaved poets: "I've never seen so many cleaned-up acts." He meant it affectionately: form requires transitive and intransitive verbs: form induces and is content. Was it Karl Shapiro who wrote that the poet "more times than not displays the manners of a corporal and the morals of a bellboy?" These are not occupational hazards but human ones.

John Ciardi complained. "The last time I was here, Johnson was president and you could drive up to the door and they had something worth drinking." He meant bourbon.

And Barbara Angelo said, explaining the 14.5 carat diamond she was wearing in a ring given to her by her husband: "When I first saw it, I told him it looked like a small skating rink. He said, 'You'll get used to it.' I did."

And speaking of getting used to it, my cancer-throttled idol and friend said to me, "God, Bill, it's good to see you." Yes indeed.

Most of us knew and liked or at least respected each other. Underneath the good fellowship the old literary enmities thrived, like the blind fish in underground rivers, but nobody was acting one out so that others had to notice. And didn't we feel honored? Yes indeed, and on behalf of not only our honored selves but also those poets and lovers of poetry who couldn't be there. Poets who might well be rancorous contestants at a summer conference or a series of readings seemed genuinely to feel that they were representatives of the activity of writing poems, of the longing that makes us write poems and of the terrifying difficulty that the activity and its traditions present all poets with.

At about 6:45, late because of the high spirits and because some guests had been passed through security as much as an hour late, the White House aides began to close the party down: "We're securing the House for the family." Guests drifted off to hotel bars, to restaurants, to dinners in the area. Though there would be snow on Friday, the bland stars shone. Off to our dinners we went.

I ate in a lovely house under the shadow of the National Cathedral (n.b., Matthew Arnold) with Dave Smith, Helen Vendler, Susan Stone, and a young novelist I'd never met who turned out to have had as an usher in his wedding a mutual crony who was best man at mine. Our shared friend is now an FM disc jockey for a rock station in Cincinnati and bears the *nom de voix* Michael Xanadu. Wine in carafes: Robert Mondavi Red Table Wine.

Talk, talk, talk. God, how we all love words. Next thing we knew it was midnight, and soon we were dispersed to our various hotels. I had a flight at 7:50 a.m.

"American poetry is somewhere / in a plane over Wyoming," wrote Auden. In the capitol it's a persistent error to confuse the office and the office-holder: it's a rare error in Auden. But then again the few poets who went to the White House were representatives, if appointed rather than elected, and in some curious and even touching way, American poetry had been honored. My seat-mate asked me if I'd been in Washington on business. "No," I said, "I was there as a civilian." Later in the same poem I quoted above, Auden wrote: "God bless America, so big / so friendly and so rich." I thought about those lines and my dying friend, and down through the clouds we came to a deft landing in a cross-wind.

# What It Means to Be American: Emily Dickinson's Home Economics

It's interesting and finally satisfying that we know little about the biographical erotic lives of Whitman and Dickinson, our two great 19th century American poets. The poems are full of testimony to the central position of the erotic in their imaginations.

We might think for a brief time on how much closer the Amherst of Dickinson's day was to the frontier than to 1988. It was still a very young society, and it rewarded men most for making it orderly. Preachers like Reverend Charles Wadsworth, with whom Dickinson carried on an intellectual friendship, were among the few men admired for being emotional or charismatic, and if he tried it outside the church he'd have seemed as odd as a bird as Whitman seemed to his contemporaries. Men like Dickinson's father and Judge Lord (another recipient of Dickinson's love letters) were like Aeneas. On the off chance that you haven't re-read *The Aeneid* lately, let me suggest a figure from popular culture who seems to have plagiarized from *The Aeneid*: Captain Kirk from *Star Trek*. Such men are duty-bound, resourceful, essentially military in values and bearing, fascinated by action and law, naturally political. They are, in short, public men, and by default private life is largely left to the women in and around their lives.

There were two more intellectual friendships important to Dickinson—one with T. W. Higginson, a contributor at *The Atlantic Monthly*, and the other with Benjamin Newton, a law student in her father's office, who urged her to take her poetic "vocation" seriously. All of these men served Dickinson as a muse; it was as if she wrote her best when she had some sympathetic spirit, a particular person in mind. It apparently didn't matter much if the muse got the poems. Higginson saw probably fifty of her poems, and there's no evidence that Lord saw more than two. The process seems to have worked this way: she began from a tenacious privacy, with of course its components of solitude and ache, and from this longing she could make connections, which we should probably imagine as being like those swinging rope bridges in the Indiana Jones movies. Across these passionate letters could pass, and poems were written that might cross, if she chose. A fulfilled love would have threatened her privacy, from which, after all, she wrote, and to which she was stubbornly and beautifully faithful.

~

Here's Dickinson's #987. She didn't give her poems titles, so the compiler of the definitive edition of her work has assigned numbers to all her poems. The date of this one is around 1865.

> The Leaves like Women interchange
> Exclusive Confidence—
> Somewhat of nods and somewhat
> Portentous influence.
>
> The Parties in both cases
> Enjoining secrecy—
> Inviolable compact
> To notoriety.

A word about Dickinson's form before we look at this short poem's deceptively off-hand argument. She wrote in hymn meter, so called, a variation on the ballad stanza. Hymn meter means what it says: in a society where church-going was usual, the rhythm was at once at one's fingertips and the prestige of being the rhythm in which God was addressed—not by the invariably male preacher, but by the congregation, with the women and children not last but singing alongside the men.

Notice that in the first stanza of Dickinson's poem no words are necessarily spoken; it's as if the women as much as the leaves speak a different language than the American English men speak. Indeed, to paraphrase Shaw's joke about Britain and America, it may well be that men and women are separated by a common language.

And let's note in the second stanza how much of Dickinson's language is legal. "The Parties in both cases" could be cut & pasted from a brief, and

"Exclusive Confidence" sounds like contract law, as does "inviolable compact." The first word of line 6, "enjoining," is meant to ring in our ears with the formal and portentous tone of legal language, and we'll miss a possibility in the last line if we fail to read "notoriety" as something a *notary* has, in addition to hearing in it the first dictionary definition. Women make up a world with unwritten but real laws, and declare the structure of that world by a language closer to the language of trees than of men.

The speed with which Dickinson can build a world from the scraps at hand—one of the fabled virtues of women in colonial New England and later on the prairies—is stunning. There's a murmur in the leaves, a dull poet would begin, much the way Snoopy begins his bad novel with the famous sentence, "It was a dark and stormy night." For long years the educational tribute to the indefatigable housewife who could build a dress or meal, if not a world, from the scraps at hand, was *home economics*. Dickinson's poem is like *home linguistics* or *home law*. Our perky housewife, or perky spinster, as Dickinson must have been categorized, must have been both proud of these magpie abilities and tired of never having richer materials to work with. Here's the short and intensely bittersweet #1755:

> To make a prairie it takes one clover and one bee,
> One clover, and a bee,
> And revery.
> The revery alone will do,
> If bees are few.

To be a woman of sensibility and passion in 19th century America was, I suspect, hard going. Bees were few. They came droning home from a day of real estate law, earnest public debates about whether or not black people had souls, and discussions of road building and taxation. They were tired. They had every reason to be tired. They were not necessarily dull men and God knows they were not necessarily bad men, and they were tired and bees were few.

Those of you who are female in the late 20$^{th}$ century will be thinking how much things have changed since Dickinson's day. Some. I think there is a tributary—in picking that word I'm thinking of how the Missouri and Ohio rivers, let's say, contribute their rich waters to the Mississippi River but, like a woman at marriage, lose their names—to the American language that is the secret language of women's loneliness, and of how women express and alleviate it, and that Dickinson, among her many other claims to our love, is the first woman writer and first woman poet to give her fellow Americans, however grudgingly and posthumously, a long look into that language.

# Martial's Darts

Martial's enemies ought to be everyone's—hypocrisy, emotional stinginess, gaud, sanctimony, prigs and dullards. The younger Pliny left an informal eulogy: "He was a man of genius, of subtle, quick intelligence, and one who in his writings showed the greatest amount of wit and pungency, and no less of fairness... " Here's what Martial said about fairness: "I spare the person, and denounce the vice."

So satirists always testify, as though they'd never based a character on someone their hippest readers would easily recognize. Fresh satire is peppered by gossip. So if the person is spared, it's sometimes because the person has, as the audience for satire tends to do, assumed that the joke's on someone else. As a recent Russian catchphrase has it, "Satires which the censor can understand are justly condemned."

Rome was a metropolis, but literary Rome was a village. Surely some in it were stung by Martial's nastiest epigrams, which comprise a pleasingly large measure of his best work. They level and deflate. There's an emotional democracy in their assumption that we're all subject to human folly, and a clear understanding of one way social life works: "For what do we live, but to make sport for our neighbors, and laugh at them in our turn?" as Mr. Bennett observes in *Pride and Prejudice*.

Of course if you lived in Martial's Rome and aspired to folly, his eye was ever on you.

It's interesting to ponder briefly how this form, in Martial's hands affable and nasty, social and suspicious of rank, became for the great British epigrammatists—Jonson, Herrick, Rochester—an essentially aristocratic form.

They did it the same way families do it. You inflate and dote on the virtues of your ancestors and then claim a pleased merit from being in the lineage. The tag "Augustan" for a period in British literature refers to a Rome no historian nor reader of Martial would recognize.

Much of literary history works this way, and is about crises of authority and status in the present rather than about the past.

"Epigram" first mean, literally enough, "written on something," e.g., a building, a statue, a grave marker. The last instance became so popular it grew its own name, "epitaph."

By extension the something on which the poem was written became an occasion or a subject, as in Jonson's "On Spies":

> Spies, you are lights in state, but of base stuff,
> Who, when you've burnt yourselves down to the snuff,
> Stink and are thrown away. End fair enough.

Martial's epigrams have no titles. They were, about 1500 of them, published in twelve books, starting in AD 84 or 85, when Martial was in his forties. He may have published apprentice work that hasn't survived. In any event, he published in AD 80 his *Liber Spectaculorum*, timed to celebrate and capitalize on the opening of the Colosseum by Titus. There were also the *Xenia* and *Apophoreta*, which need not concern us here except that their publication, probably in AD 84 or 85, had made him popular and cocky enough to joke about it, however hopefully. Here's the first epigram in Book I:

> Here he is whom you read and clamor for,
> tasteful reader, the very Martial world-
> renowned for pithy books of epigrams
> and not even dead yet. So seize your chance:
> better to praise him when he can hear
> than later, when he'll be literature.

This was to become a familiar theme. Here's V, x:

> Why is it modern poets are ignored
> and only dead ones get adored?
> That's how envy works, Regulus,

>    the dead make the safest rivals.
>    So we mourn Pompey's colonnade
>    and its nostalgic, leafy shade
>    just as our fathers praised the temple
>    Catulus restored not wisely nor too well.
>    Rome reads Ennius, though Virgil is to hand,
>    as Homer was a joke in his own land.
>    Menander's best plays were thought dull;
>    only Corinna knew her Ovid well.
>    So, little books, let's not rush to our fate.
>    Since death comes before glory, let's be late.

That's not the poet Catullus, with two "l"s, by the way, but the consul (elevated in BC 105) Catulus, one "l," an apparatchik with a love of building projects.

Martial was born in Bilbilis, in Hispania Terraconensis (modern Spain) sometime from AD 38 to 41. His dates are murky. As one historian has it, "His death cannot be dated later than AD 104." He came to Rome for the usual reasons—he was restless, it was cosmopolitan.

Was he married? Did he have children? Probably not, but his life, as a narrative, is murky. There are a few epigrams in which he speaks in the first person of family life, but our very word "person" comes from the Latin *personare* (*per*, through; *sonare*, to sound): the large-mouthed masks actors wore on the Roman stage were named from the voices sounding through them. You are who you act is a satirist's credo.

He lived thirty-five years in Rome, and led, according to one of his translators, Walter Ker, "the ordinary life of the needy client dependent on rich patrons, and he never ceases to complain of the weariness of levees to be attended, complimentary duties to be discharged at unreasonable hours and in all weathers, and of the insolence and stinginess of wealthy men."

For part of those years in Rome there was a legislated dole, a kind of minimum wage for clients. Clients were hired retinue: they'd provide company, use their signet rings to witness documents, liven the dinner table, be amiable on demand, etc. They had, let's say, the relationship to their patrons that teaching writers have to the sufferance of the English department.

A few clients made out like bandits; think of Horace's Sabine Farm. Most of them got by, more or less.

On the other hand, as Ker notes, "he was not without compensations." Domitian rejected a petition for money, but Titus, whose Colosseum Martial limned, conferred on him rights and titles—much valued in rank-besotted Rome—, and his friends included Quintillian, the younger Pliny, and Juvenal.

Martial had, in short, the usual class situation of the successful writer: a tenacious and vocal loyalty to humble beginnings, and a mute and tenacious pleasure in proud company.

And in this he had the usual mixed feelings. Here's V, lvi:

> You wonder, Lupus, who's the best schoolmaster
> for your son? To skirt certain disaster,
> strike from your list all teachers of grammar
> and rhetoric. Have him wholly ignore
> anything by Cicero, and Virgil, too.
> Read Tutilius? Tutilius who?
> If the boy should scribble a few verses,
> disinherit him. He could do far worse
> than learn to make money—to play the harp
> or tootle a flute. If he's no too sharp,
> don't mope. It takes but paltry intellect
> to be an auctioneer or architect.

The allusion to Tutilius in the line after one that brandishes Cicero and Virgil is probably ironic. Few can answer the question today, but then? Substitute for the name of the horse in X, ix, the name of Secretariat, or Ed McMahon, a veteran of the client/patron relationship.

> Martial, moralist and wit,
> a household name in sixty houses!
> Don't envy me. I'm less famous
> than Andraemon, the horse, is.

Is fame the issue? Martial asks, who said "world-renowned" in I, i. Which of him do you believe? As Zoot Sims described Stan Getz, "he's a nice bunch of guys."

Some of the epigrams are literary barbs. Here's VII, xc:

> Matho calls my epigrams "uneven;"
> from him, I count that praise.
> The stuff he likes is consistent, all right:
> smooth torpor, constant daze.

And here's XI, xciii:

> Ted's studio burnt down, with all his poems.
> Have the Muses hung their heads?
> You bet, for it was criminal neglect
> not also to have sautéed Ted.

VII, iv is an insouciant literary epitaph.

> He paled, he wrote some poems, white heat:
> etc. Then he grew worse.
> Does travel to the last resort
> always leave an exhaust of verse?

You'll see from the exhaust metaphor that I've been a little insouciant myself in regard to anachronisms in my translations. My main impulse has not been curatorial, but to see what Martial would sound like if he lived in his Rome and wrote in my American English.

Roman marriages were complicated business, mergers first and foremost. In this deeply patriarchal society free women had access to divorce and could, at that point, retrieve their dowries. Here's I, x:

> Gemellus burns to marry Maronilla.
> He pleads, he begs, he launches fleets of gifts.

> Is she so beautiful? No, she's a hag.
> So what's the lure? Her cough. It's deep. She's rich.

Or X, xliii:

> Phileros, that makes seven
> wives you've buried on your land.
> Sow the body, read the estate:
> isn't agriculture grand?

And here's VIII, xliii:

> Fabius buries his wives
> and Chrestilla her husbands;
> the soft lights in their bedrooms
> flare from a funeral torch.
> Venus, you've outdone yourself:
> at last, the finalists contend.
> Expect a double funeral
> if they both run true to form.

Of course these crass opportunists had maintenance work to do between the wedding and probate. Here's IX, lxxx:

> Gellius was so starved and poor
> he found a rich and aged wife.
> How does Gellius mind the store?
> He dines, then fucks her for dear life.

And here's VI, xlvii:

> Your Celia keeps company with eunuchs:
> Pannychus, do you find this odd?
> It's the child she wishes to be spared,
> Pannychus, not the rod.

Martial saw sex, like marriage, as essentially a transaction, and the best spectator's sport to be had from it was deciding if it was a good deal or not. Here's IX, xxi:

> Art and Cal have made a trade:
> Art's land for Cal's young slave.
> Who's the winner? Hard to guess:
> they're both plowing new furrows.

Tenderness in romantic matters is not a common tone in Martial; perhaps his own experience of it came late. In Book XII, sent to Rome for publication from Spain, where Martial had returned for his last years, there's a touching poem addressed to Marcella, who seems to have worried that the urban cynic would long for the moil of Rome. Not so, he assures in the final line of XII, xxi:

> You, by yourself, comprise a Rome for me.

This is far from the earlier and more common tone of III, liii:

> Could I give up your neck, Chloe, your face,
> your hands and lips, those breasts, those legs, those flanks?
> Don't ask. No need to list the parts. It's all
> of you I could dispense with, Chloe. Thanks.

There's an interesting note of distaste at the center of Martial's tone in many of his erotic epigrams, and it's not possible to say how much of it comes from his attitudes toward erotic life itself and how much from his dismay how much willful self-deception we blink when the fires are high. Here's V, lxxxiii:

> You're hot to trot? Well then I'm not.
> You've cooled. I'm ardent on the spot.
> What's going on? Don't sulk, my pet:
> I like you best as hard to get.

III, xc is not cheerful:

> She's half a mind to sleep with me,
> half a mind to not.
> Unfortunately half a mind is all
> that Galla's got.

In VI, xxvi, a very emblematic poem, the contempt is perhaps more accurately directed.

> Papylus had a dong so long
> and a nose so vast and subtle
> that when it reared its ugly head
> Papylus could smell trouble.

And there's the very interesting poem, VII, xii, which has usually been translated with a slightly leering, boys-will-be-boys tone. I hear something more plaintive.

> Why don't I yearn to wed a rich wife?
> I'd give up the key to my will and heart.
> A man should begin firmly in power
> if he can't be equal without a head start.

More than any of the models for the lampooned characters in the epigrams, we might well surmise, Martial was chastened by them.

But his healthy rancor never subsided, not his delight in the complex and often lurid social life he enjoyed and mined for material. The insolence of money is Martial's pilot light from beginning to end. Here's X, xxxi:

> You sold a slave just yesterday
> for twelve hundred sesterces, Cal;
> at last the lavish dinner you've
> long dreamed about is in the pan.

> Tonight! Fresh mullet, four full pounds!
> You know I'll not complain, old pal,
> about the food. But that's no fish
> we'll eat tonight; that was a man.

Patrons were expected to feed their clients regularly and clients were quick to complain about the stinting, as in X, xlix:

> Although you fill amethyst cups
> with wine even more rare, you pour
> for me a Sabine wine not three months
> off the lees. Worse, this jejune dread
> arrives in a gold cup. What for,
> Cotta? The stuff is liquid lead.

Of the many direct appeals Martial filed for money needed to be artful, this is my favorite (VI, lxxxii):

> Someone we both know, Rufus, looked me
> up and down the other day, as if I
> were a novice gladiator. "Can you,"
> he wryly wanted to know, "be the Martial
> whose snide, metallic poems everyone knows
> who's not deaf to a joke?" What could I say?
> I smiled, I bowed, I did not lie. "Why then,"
> he asked—his trap had sprung—"your shockingly
> bad cloak?" "It's all my verse has earned," I had
> to tell him. Rufus, save us both from this
> embarrassment: Buy me a decent cloak.

The implicit promise of future beneficence built into the patron/client relationship was morally corrosive to both parties, of course, but grated materially on the client, day after day, and Martial's XII, xl is a magnificent cry of pent rage:

> You lie and I concur. You "give"
> a reading of your wretched verse
> and I applaud. You sing and I
> too lift my blowsy voice.
>
> You drink, Pontificus, and I
> drink up. You fart; I look away.
> Produce a cribbage board; I'll find
> a chance to lose, to pay.
>
> There's but one thing you do without me
> and my lips are sealed. Yet not
> a minim of your money's trickled
> down to me. So what?
>
> You'll be good to me in your will?
> No doubt you'd bounce a check from hell.
> So don't hold back on my account;
> if die you must, farewell.

There have been few skilled practitioners of the epigram since the great Augustans, but two should be cited, and by example.

This is Walter Savage Landor:

> Thy skin is like an unwashed carrot's.
> Thy tongue is blacker than a parrot's.
> Thy teeth are crooked, but belong
> Inherently to such a tongue.

And this is J. V. Cunningham:

> I had gone broke, and got set to come back,
> And lost, on a hot day and a fast track,

> On a long shot at long odds, a black mare
> By Hatred out of Envy by Despair.

It's too bad Cunningham didn't translate more Martial than he did. His version of IV, lxix is so perfect I didn't try one:

> You serve the best wines always, my dear sir,
> And yet they say your wines are not so good.
> They say you are four times a widower.
> They say ... A drink? I don't believe I would.

It took Arthur Rubinstein five days (four in December, 1965, and one in January, 1966) to record the 51 Chopin mazurkas, which you or I can now buy on two RCA CDs. The Chopin lover's heart applauds this tidy package, but it will melt his attention to sludge if he goes straight home and listens to them all straight through.

Surely epigrams are the same. Maybe even this brief talk has seemed a barrage, though of course I hope not. Book I had 118 epigrams, and I'll let the last of them serve us as an ending:

> If a hundred epigrams won't fill you up,
> then no amount of swill will brim your cup.

# Shortages

A teenaged boy and a power mower make a stolid force against the encroachment of meadow. The boy mowing the lawn of our rented summerhouse is implacable and dreamy at once. It seems as though nothing in the exact moment can touch him, though years later, when he seldom strips to the waist outdoors except to swim, the aroma of cut grass will send across his loosening skin like a breeze the combined prickle of grassflecks and sweat. Probably it will lie just beyond the farthest reach of speech, like so much of the body's memory—crowded, opaque and mute. How long ago that was, he might think, though how long can time be if he can be blown across it, say thirty years of it, like a crinkle of paper across a city street? Even if he had greater than usual linguistic powers he would struggle and struggle, and most days fall back, fall short, failing to tug back by its frayed leash of a name another component of those swarming odors thirty years ago. But on a rare day he might find it, hidden a little shyly in the throng like his shadowy, eye-lowered cousin who hid for a few years her reticent, oval and wholly beautiful face in the back row of the family's group photographs, and then fled to Albuquerque. Suddenly there's a faint tug on the other end, and now he's got it! The odor of a single crushed mulberry.

∽

Every year The Ausable Club, a WASP bastion in St. Hubert's, NY, ignites a fireworks display for the townspeople. This year, 1989, the rockets go up on July 2. We all sit on the fairway of the club's finishing hole and look up and chatter. Here are some scraps of overheard conversation.

> #1:
> Clubmember: Those goddamn kids are running across the greens.
> His wife: You say that every year.
> Clubmember: They do it every goddamn year.

#2:

Wife: Look, there's a scrap from that last firework, still burning.

Husband: It's probably a shooting star or a satellite.

Wife: They say the shooting stars here are beautiful.

Husband: It's more likely to be a satellite.

Wife: What?

Husband: That thing you saw.

Wife: Oh. Well, if a satellite fell, could you see it?

Husband: Sure.

Wife: Have you ever seen one?

Husband: How would I know?

#3:

Townsperson 1: Look at that clubhouse, will you? What do you think they do in there?

Townsperson 2: They don't talk about money.

Townsperson 1: That's all?

Townsperson 2: That's a lot.

~

One morning two women in their sixties come to the door. One stands a half step behind the other, who's the spokeswoman. "We're the Peck girls," she announces, "and we came here long ago."

She looks around a little wanly, for she's not sure, as it turns out, just where "here" was. The land here is no longer farmed, and though it's been in the same family for years, there have been marriages enough that none of the current owners of the three houses on the family compound bear the same names as the many dead in the family cemetery behind the house we're renting.

"We used to stay in a kind of dormitory," she explains, "over there," and where she waved her arm there's now a field hidden from the road by a scraggly clump of lilac bushes, and behind the field there's a woodlot blurring toward disuse, and behind it a meander of the Ausable River.

"We loved it here," she begins, and then there's a dithery hitch in her conversational momentum, a tiny coquettish fidget that's very girlish indeed, and in just that instant I can imagine her standing in the orchard to the northwest of the house, turning an apple in her hands, one eye on it and another avid to see if she were being watched.

"And so we've come back." I churlishly fear an onslaught of narrative. Summers I fiercely protect the right to waste my own time. But I'm wrong. She's found all the story she could or would tell me. "We loved it here and so we've come back."

∼

Keene Valley is beautiful and thus many people want to be buried there. But the summer people, who, in the way of things, can more easily afford them, bought up gravesites so eagerly that people who had invested in the town the hard, year-round living that earns a gravesite began to fear there would be none left for them. And so it was ruled that nobody who didn't own land in Keene Valley or live there year-round could buy a gravesite.

One day a rich man flew over town in his Cessna and thought, "My God, this is beautiful; I wonder if I could buy a gravesite here." He landed and asked his way to the town hall, only to be told of the new rule. So he strode across the road to a local realtor's office, bought one acre of land, strode back across the road, bought a gravesite, and strode back across the road to put his acre up for sale, and then he flew away.

Perhaps, then, it would be most effective to end this stockpiling of gravesites by a rule harder to circumvent. In the future, no gravesite would be sold to the living. When residents or people who owned land in Keene Valley died, their heirs could purchase a gravesite in their behalves.

Picture, then, the wrath of a man who had been away while this new rule was angrily written in the wake of the morbid aviator's triumph over the previous rule, and who dropped by the town hall, as he'd been promising himself for three years now he would, to purchase a gravesite. He's a widower, without children. As the rule is now written, he can't buy a gravesite and can't imagine, at least today, when he bursts into the Noonmark Diner to rant and redden before a few of his townspeople, how he'll ever contrive to have what he calls, quite straightforwardly, his birthright. That was five minutes into his tirade, which took fifteen. He's finished now, and leaving, kicking a knob or two of gravel as he strides across the parking lot to his dusty car, and someone inside the Noonmark is saying to another, "You know, for a minute there I thought he was gonna need one this very afternoon."

※

The tabloids near the checkout counters at the Grand Union in Lake Placid report, week after week, sightings of Elvis, but among the intellectual classes in the valley, bear is the local *yeti*. The summer produces one authentic sighting. "It was a male," the male who spotted him says confidently. Probably. There will be photographs to speculate about, for the man called his wife and she rushed from an afternoon shower to stand, naked, on the roof of their porch, shielded by woods from view of any other humans, and snapped a few pictures of him as he ambled from the woods on one side of their driveway into the woods on the other side.

Other bear sightings are reported in local bars, where, here as anywhere, stories get enlarged and cropped. "He must have weighed six hundred pounds," says someone of the only bear she claims ever to have seen. "We stood and looked at each other for a while. I was rooted to the spot. There was no tree to climb." If this anecdote ever passes from oral tradition into written form, there's a nearly irresistible opportunity in the proximity of "rooted" and "tree" that only a fine writer could forego.

Another adventure goes like this. A capable outdoorsman is asleep in a tent, in a mummy bag so that only his face is uncovered. In fact he's rather tightly bundled into a bag little larger than the one in which he, a former naval officer, might have been buried at sea in a crueler and shorter life. There's a clatter just outside his tent, where earlier he'd cooked a rudimentary camper's dinner. Through the flap of his tent pokes, with a what-have-we-here? twitch about it, a bearnose. He lies still in his bag. He tries to breathe as silently as he can.

Both anecdotes end the same way. Bear and human are close enough for swift and violent trouble, fear fills the human like a glass, and the bear, unaccountably, withdraws, leaving in the space behind it a burgeoning story.

It would not do to poke these stories. Six hundred pounds is a measure of something, but something in the storyteller; heavyweight local bears weigh in at two hundred. Why is the female anecdotalist sure the bear was male? And, why a mummy bag, except in winter, when bears are denned in?

A bear in the woods is a bear, but a bear on the edge of human lives is a story.

―

In his biography of Freud, Peter Gay, using Freud's daybooks as source material, notes that in Freud's later years he annually recorded his non-receipt of the Nobel Prize, for which he had every reason to think himself a strong candidate in either medicine or literature. Of course everything in his temperament, experience and clinical practice would lead him to cite the anniversaries of deprivations, those precious vacuums the psyche abhors. Each year Freud, ever and in this case perhaps unconsciously the good Jew, would jot, "Passed over for the Nobel again."

―

Two of the summer's blockbuster movies depend, for the shared assumptions that link them to their huge audiences, on the explicit premise that New York City is seething, like a diabolic battery or a hive of vile and moiling honey, with malevolence; the city is awash with more longing, anger and injustice than it can contain or transform.

Who can redeem such a place?

In *Batman*, Bruce Wayne, a dicty WASP with an inherited fortune, no living relatives, a repressed crush on his boy ward and a closetful of batdrag, surges into the lurid streets in his Batmobile, a vehicle descended equally from the boomerang, the pimpmobile and the limousine with smoked glass windows in which William F. Buckley, Jr., is driven from Connecticut to work. In

*Ghostbusters II*, a gang of amiable fuck-ups, in an inspired parody of New Age credulity, manipulate the occult with gadgetry.

In the issues of *The New York Times* I drive to Keene each morning to buy there are stranger and harsher stories. In Alabama a black man with an IQ of 68 has been electrocuted for vicious crimes. Thousands of pages of legal briefs have been written about his case, and we might well imagine them piled on either side of him and forming a long corridor at the end of which "the people of the state of Alabama," as the enabling documents for execution conventionally say, will kill him. He was strapped into an electric chair and a lethal dose of electricity was run through his body. But he didn't die. The *Times* didn't say how much the worse he was for this wear. The people of the state of Alabama had to do it all over again. It took nineteen minutes to kill this murderer and rapist. Pressed for an explanation of this inefficiency, the warden ascribed it to "human error."

A middle-aged man from the Washington, DC, area rented a small plane, filed a flight plan for Charlotte, NC, and then radioed in to say that he was feeling faint. Military aircraft followed his six hour flight. In his cabin, first reports had it, he could be seen slumped over the controls. His plane ran out of fuel and crashed at sea in the Caribbean. He was rescued alive, all the more a source for wonder when it became apparent that he had a gunshot wound in his stomach. How could this have happened? He'd been carrying a handgun in the plane's equivalent of a glove compartment and it must have gone off on impact, he guessed. Medical people who examined him said, however, that the shot had been fired from even closer and probably several hours before the plane crashed. A later report from one of the military pilots who had monitored his flight said he'd been seen to move in his seat. It turns out he was a lawyer who represented clients before a governmental agency that required elaborate procedures for licensing, and that he'd accepted fees from so large a number of clients that he must have known he couldn't get each client's application heard during current sessions. One of the lawyers who was his frequent opponent at these hearings told the press, "We knew he was over-committed, so we papered him to death," filing motion after motion and brief after brief. Given the likelier outcome of the pilot's adventure, the phrase "papered him to death" would be like saying, in regard to the black man executed in Alabama, "more power to you." There's no available end to this story for now, as it will wind up in one or more courts and none of the lawyers involved is talking to the press.

Of course there's no end, except that a murderer's victim and now that victim's murderer are dead, to the Alabama story.

There is a movie out this summer not about whether or not New York can work, but about a few fictional characters there. Spike Lee's *Do The Right Thing* is set in New York, which is not in this case, by a kind of metonymy-in-reverse, a way to say "Manhattan." The film is set in Brooklyn. Suppose someone told you that *Do The Right Thing* is the best American movie about how black and white people do and don't get along since. . . You fill in the blank. How long will it take you?

～

In the post office a woman asks the postmaster how to get to a nearby flume. "Flumes?" the postmaster muses. "There must be about twenty. We don't bother about them."

"There's a beautiful photograph of one by Nathan Farb," the woman says, "and it made me want to see it." To her Farb is a famous photographer.

"A photographer," the postmaster thinks; "it makes sense. He gets a lot of stiff mail."

～

One night the Keene Valley Public Library hosts a reading by Russell Banks from his new novel, *Affliction*, which is about male violence, child beating, small town politics, despair and a man murdered during deer season in upstate New Hampshire.

By reading's end the ample crowd that came out on a rainy summer night to hear Banks read about such brutal and depressing matters is oddly exhilarated, as if an open-eyed meeting with life at its nastiest were somehow tonic. A few of us drift across the road to the Ausable Inn for a drink.

There's talk of bears, the cloudy procedures by which long marriages survive, the shortness of summer.

I ask a friendly and sad-faced painter with whom I sometimes play tennis about his grown children, three sons. One wants to live at home, another wants to found a rock group in New Orleans, and the third, the good son, has taken a job he's slowly learning to hate. "There's something they think I didn't give them, and they don't know what it is, and it makes them angry." He pauses a minute." And there's something I didn't give them, and I don't know what it is, and it makes me depressed."

There's a longer pause. "Tennis tomorrow?" he asks. "You bet," I say.

None of our jokes about swift time and short summers has stayed the pace one whit, and suddenly the walks and dinners and hours of uninterrupted work and tennis matches will be used up wholly.

At summer's end I have an elaborate and populous dream from which I wake holding onto only one tiny fragment:

I'm sitting on a wall. A big German shepherd, very like but also recognizably not a beloved shepherd I lived with for twelve years, trots over to me and starts to leap up at me, snuffling and whimpering the way a dog greets you when you've been gone longer than usual. But the wall is too high. He can't really get his paws to my chest or his muzzle to mine. So he slinks off. I turn to the person sitting next to me on the wall and say, in a voice which even in the dream I know to be uncomfortably like the teacher's voice I'm about to speak in again for a living, "The tragedy of dogs is that they can't fuck humans."

The idea of a *vacation*, something *vacant*, is no tension. But we hate that. The bears come out of the woods, the kids are snarky or have won a battle over the lurking snarkiness in their murky natures, a relative of the landlord comes by to borrow a tool from the barn and we emit as he leaves a small blue flame of loathing for his violation of our fiction that this rented place is ours for the summer. If there's tension, we can talk about it.

Of course I'm a writer, so what's a vacation to me? Summers I work. Today I'm a little tired and the deteriorating socket in my left hip broadcasts dull pain steadily. I think morosely of half-lives and decay. The baby apples in the orchard are no bigger than table tennis balls. I think of a passage from Ovid in which the envious shades in the underworld stand around and talk, like high school athletes, about the good old days. "Remember the smell of apples?" one asks.

The way wine subsides in a particularly good bottle, such as one might drink for a birthday or with good friends, time empties me of itself. I play a computer game for three hours and win. That's tension. What's for dinner?

---

If you should have a hip replacement operation, they measure you before they table you, and the last thing they do before they're done with this now rather routine procedure is to measure you again, so that they can restore, exactly, the uneven lengths of your two legs, so that when you wooze out of bed and stand for the first time on post-operative legs, one revised and one the same as ever, you feel not the shock of symmetry but the ease and slur of familiar imperfection. "Calipers," the surgeon commands. "Mallet." Then "calipers" again. "All right," he says, "this guy's done." He's got two operations after lunch.

---

What's for dinner? I've made lemon and pepper fettucine, tossed it with chopped fresh plum tomatoes, minced fresh basil, a handful of ground pignoli, some olive oil, a suspicion of balsamic vinegar. There are roasted yellow peppers on the side. I've made peach ice cream for dessert and opened two bottles of 1978 Grumello. There are more in reserve.

Then, whatever it is, it flies through the kitchen. A bat? One woman touches her hair. A swallow? They wheel and dip from the barn across the rented lawn and back into the barn. Maybe a swallow has blundered into the house, attached here to the barn in wary honor of the long winters.

I've been at work in the kitchen for an hour and I'm hungry, I want wine, I want to be praised and loved for cooking so well, I want everyone at the table grateful and articulate as the day drains through the colander of dusk and the shadows of the candles grow starker.

So we seal it off, whatever it is, room by room. We close the doors from the dining room to the sitting room, and then from the sitting room to the front hall. From there it can fly only upstairs. Then we close the doors to each of the upstairs rooms, so that is has only the upstairs hallway, at the open end of which may be the path it might refind to the barn, if that's how it got in.

Five minutes spent on all this, we go downstairs to eat.

Whatever it was, we can't find it after dinner and the next day we can't find it and we declare it gone.

A few nights later five of us who were there for dinner the night it flew through have a good natured argument about whether a bat can detect by echo-location the crossed strings of a tennis racket. If not, you could stun a bat with a racket and pick it up crumpled and carry it, like a pizza on one of those long-handled paddles they use in pizza parlors, and deposit it outdoors, where it would eventually ungrog and unfurl and fly off. But if so, one of us who was there the night it flew through, whatever it was, but who's not here tonight, was, we agree, lying through his teeth.

This person who may or may not be lying through his teeth, it should be clearly understood, is someone we love. Nobody talks about fear of bats and nobody in this rather over-educated group mentions the famous passage in Old English where a sparrow flies through the mead hall, in a window at one end and out a window at the other, a willed but fervent emblem for how short life is, and perhaps even for how little it matters, when life is that short, how long art is.

# Poetic License

When I was teaching myself to cook, I was also teaching myself to write poems. In those days I didn't compare the two ancient and related crafts but simply slogged along, useful mistake by useful mistake.

The first poems I wanted to write would have been, had I the requisite skill, exactly like the poems I most admired. But it would be a slow process indeed, by which I struggled from clumsy imitation to invention, to a point where I wrote poems that, for better or for worse, only I could have written.

Similarly, in the kitchen I hoped to make what I most liked to eat. But this ambition required culinary skills with names I barely knew. I was a bookish youth, and so I set out for the bookstore. *Joy of Cooking* would help, I thought.

It did, but it can also terrify. The novice, hubris in heart and whisk in hand, stares rather gloomily at this sentence from "About Dessert Souffles": "If the egg whites are under- or overbeaten, they have the look and texture of an old leather belt."

"About Dessert Souffles" refers the reader to "About Souffles," which gives a list of disasters that can—you'll pardon the verb—befall a souffle. Crucial points are preceded by an admonitory black arrow. Here's one: "If your electric oven has a top element, be sure to remove it, as the heat is often enough to stiffen the top surface of the souffle too quickly..."

It was bad enough that I had no idea what under- or overbeaten egg whites looked and felt like, and now the cookbook was advising me to disassemble my oven.

"If you can read," I had told myself, "you can cook." But I hadn't anticipated from *Joy of Cooking* such a prophetic, chastising, Isaiah-like tone.

Trial and error, the only method of thought I've ever known, solved the problem of the egg whites, and fear of taking appliances apart solved the other.

And I came to admire in *Joy of Cooking* a kind of scorched-earth poetry and a nearly drunken mixture of dictions. Consider this passage, the beginning of "About Dried Legumes": "Dried peas and beans, being rather on the dull side, much like dull people respond readily to the right contacts. Do not scorn them, for they have valuable, if incomplete, proteins, see page 2."

A souffle breathes glamour and adds a loud whisper of seductive intent to a meal prepared for a friend, but I needed and wanted to learn to cook more daily fare. My cookbook shelf expanded, and I worked my way through standard preparations. I'd make the full recipe, though I seldom had but one or two to feed, and then experiment with the leftovers. One's life as a cook changes the day he first "invents" something. All I did was combine aspects of two recipes in order to make do with a scant larder, but I'd found a way to start from a cookbook rather than always end there.

The cookbooks I'd once been glad to follow slavishly seemed now a cache of themes awaiting variation. And I learned to quarrel with them. "Serves six," a recipe says cheerfully—six elves, perhaps, but my guests were full-size. "Cook until the onions are clear," recipe after recipe advises, but who not influenced by the great tradition of cookbook prose would describe the properly nacreous, mother-of-pearly color as "clear?" "One-quarter cup white wine" is not a helpful suggestion, since that much white zinfandel will make a risotto taste as if cream soda has been spilled into it; the recipe should specify dry white wine. But learning to argue a little with his elders and betters is part of a youngster's fun.

That cookbook shelf is by now a seven-foot high bookcase, and is crammed full. I make a souffle now and again, especially since I've discovered that if you know what the real oven temperature is when the dial says 350, a souffle is absolutely foolproof. But mostly I like to find or invent dishes that are perhaps stylish and at least comparatively simple. Faites simple, Escoffier decreed, and probably the tyro cook should inscribe that motto on the handle of his whisk.

There are human skills that we don't learn largely by imitation—how to make love, for example—but they are few. And one can imitate from books, for reading is the best imitation of experience.

A cook can do worse than play in the kitchen at imitating dishes first tasted in a restaurant. The corn salad recipe given here was, in its earliest incarnation, an attempt to duplicate a dish at Mike's American Bar and Grill, the aggressively informal bistro on Tenth Avenue in

Manhattan; the cumin has survived in each new variation, but the mayonnaise dropped out long ago. The pepper shrimp has come some distance from the Chinese dish I first imitated. The beef-and-lentil salad was once a variation on an Elizabeth David recipe for using the leftover beef from a pot-au-feu but has undergone many a furbishing since.

## Corn Salad

2 20-ounce packages frozen corn kernels
1 cup chopped scallions, both green and white parts
2/3 cup chopped pimentos
1/2 cup red-wine vinegar
1/4 cup Dijon-style mustard
2 tablespoons honey
2 teaspoons minced garlic
1 teaspoon dried thyme
1 teaspoon ground cumin
1 tablespoon salt
Freshly ground pepper to taste
1 cup olive oil
1/4 cup chopped fresh coriander

1. Cook the frozen corn according to instructions. Drain.

2. In a large bowl, combine the corn with the scallions and pimentos.

3. In a separate bowl, whisk together the vinegar, mustard, honey, garlic, thyme, cumin, salt and pepper. Add the oil in a steady stream, whisking constantly until the mixture is emulsified. Pour the dressing over the salad, add the coriander and toss until well mixed.

Yield: Eight servings.

## Penne Strascinata

6 tablespoons olive oil
1 pound dried penne
1 medium onion, chopped
1/3 cup Cognac
5 cups simmering beef stock
1 cup mushrooms, sliced
3/4 cup heavy cream
Salt to taste, if desired
2/3 cup grated Parmesan
1/2 cup parsley leaves, chopped fine
Freshly ground pepper to taste

1. In a large skillet, heat 4 tablespoons of the olive oil over moderate heat. Add the pasta and cook, stirring, until it begins to brown, about 12 to 15 minutes. Remove the pasta and set aside. Saute the onion in the remaining 2 tablespoons of oil in the skillet until soft but not brown, about 5 minutes.

2. Return the pasta to the skillet, stir in the Cognac and cook until the liquid is evaporated.

3. Add 2 cups of the beef stock and cook, stirring, until it is absorbed. Add 2 more cups stock and, when it is almost absorbed, stir in the mushrooms. Add the remaining stock 1/2 cup at a time and cook, stirring, until it is absorbed and the pasta is al dente.

4. Stir in the cream and salt and simmer until slightly thickened, about 1 minute. Remove from the heat and stir in the Parmesan. Sprinkle with parsley and pepper.

Yield: Six servings.

*Note: I can't remember where my recipe for penne strascinata came from. I seem to have entered it into the computer without stopping to puzzle over the name. In any event, the pasta is cooked much as rice is for a risotto. Broth is added at intervals so that the penne absorbs it and the result is as tasty as it is unusual.*

## Pepper Shrimp

1/2 cup fruity red wine, such as Beaujolais or red zinfandel
1 8-ounce can tomato sauce
1 teaspoon dried chervil
1 tablespoon lemon juice
1 teaspoon dry mustard
1 teaspoon dried oregano
Salt to taste
2 teaspoons pepper
1/2 cup olive oil
2 cloves garlic, minced
1/2 cup loosely packed flat-leaved parsley, chopped
2 pounds medium shrimps, peeled and deveined

1. In a bowl, whisk together the wine, tomato sauce, chervil, lemon juice, mustard, oregano, salt and pepper.

2. Heat the oil in a skillet and cook the minced garlic over medium heat for 1 minute. Add the tomato-sauce mixture and bring to a boil, then lower the heat and simmer the mixture, stirring occasionally, for 10 minutes.

3. Remove from heat and set aside to cool for 5 minutes. Stir in chopped parsley.

4. Place the shrimp in a single layer in a nonmetal baking dish. Pour the sauce over the shrimp and marinate, covered, for 3 hours at room temperature, or overnight in the refrigerator.

5. Preheat the broiler. Broil the shrimps about 6 inches from the heat for 10 minutes or until cooked through, turning once

Yield: Eight servings.

## Scallion Risotto

6 cups homemade chicken broth (or use 4 cups canned with 2 cups water)
6 tablespoons unsalted butter
1 1/4 cup chopped scallions (use the lower white and light green parts)
1 1/2 cups Arborio rice
1/2 cup dry white wine
1/3 cup chopped scallions (use the green tops)
1/2 cup grated Parmesan or grana cheese
White pepper to taste

1. In a large saucepan, bring the broth to a boil; lower the heat and keep at a scant simmer.

2. Meanwhile, in a large saute pan (see note) heat 4 tablespoons of the butter and cook the white parts of the scallions, stirring until they're soft, about 2 minutes. Add the rice, stirring with a wooden spoon, until all the grains are coated with butter. Add the wine and cook the mixture at a low simmer, stirring until all the wine is absorbed, about 3 to 4 minutes.

3. Add 1/2 cup of the simmering broth and continue to simmer the mixture, stirring until the broth is absorbed. Keep adding broth by the 1/2 cup and repeating as above until the rice is creamy and al dente. The rice may not absorb all the broth, so it's best to taste the mixture before adding the last 1/2 cup.

4. Remove the pan from the heat and stir in the remaining 2 tablespoons butter, the green scallion tops, cheese and white pepper.

Yield: Six servings as a first course, or 4, if the guests are polite, for an entree.

Note: Most risotto recipes call for the mixture to be cooked in a large saucepan, but in a large-enough saute pan the process is easier to monitor and margnially faster.

## Cold-Beef-and-Lentil Salad

2 cups lentils
5 cups water
1/4 cup balsamic vinegar
White pepper to taste
1 1/3 cup olive oil
1 pound cold flank steak, cooked medium to medium-rare and cut into bite-size pieces
2 bunches watercress (about 6 cups), stems removed
1 teaspoon minced garlic
1/2 cup minced scallions
1/4 cup drained capers
1/4 cup chopped sweet pickles.

1. Place the lentils and the water in a saucepan. Bring to a boil, then lower the heat and simmer, partly covered, until the lentils are barely tender, about 20 to 25 minutes. Drain.

2. In a small bowl, combine the vinegar and white pepper. Add the olive oil in a steady stream, whisking constantly until the mixture is emulsified.

3. In a large serving bowl, toss together the steak, lentils, watercress, garlic, scallions, capers and sweet pickles with the dressing.

Yield: Eight servings.

# REVIEWS

# William Stafford's Whetstone

"The farther he went the farther home grew," William Stafford wrote of Daniel Boone. Stafford had a penchant for the epigrammatic:

> In scenery I like flat country.
> In life I don't like much to happen.

and

> you can usually be free some of the time
> if you wake up before other people.

In another poem, Aunt Mabel says of a bellicose senator, ". . . He's a brilliant man, / but we didn't elect him that much."

He disliked pomp and swagger and had a sure sense of the heartbreak and drama in "ordinary" lives. He wrote of Kansas as ". . . the state I liked, where little happened / and much was understood." "State" here could also mean a state of mind.

Last April, The Poetry Society of America awarded Stafford its Robert Frost Medal. There are some interesting parallels between the two. Both were widely beloved poets who wrote accessible and often genial poems, though each was, in Frost's sly understatement, "acquainted with the dark." Both developed public personas that put audiences and students at ease, and both had a fierce competitive distaste for Mandarinism and elegance, specifically in their own poems and generally in literary life.

Fancy talk about writing and aesthetics set Stafford's teeth on edge. He has a small poem called "People with Whetstones."

> Hard-working hunters beyond the taiga
> sharpen their knives, get up
> early, watch carefully. They

> have a name for everyone else:
> "People who talk about God."

Stafford was interested in God—he worked for The Church of the Brethren and was a CO in World War II. It's talk about God that was unseemly to Stafford, who also got up early, watched carefully and sharpened his knife against "people who talk about God."

Stafford not only got up early, he also wrote a poem every morning; he had a whetstone. He admired others for whom work was a religious ritual—Native Americans, farmers, all folks diligent and taciturn. Notice how in these lines from "Juncos" the birds are made working class:

> Specialists on branch ends,
> craft union. I like their
> clean little coveralls.

A drab, rote correctness crept into some of the poems:

> Wisdom is having things right in your life
> and knowing why.

Some others are spoiled by Stafford's impersonation of a wise rube, a kind of avuncular Pa Kettle:

> The flat people in magazines hear
> the flat god of their tabletop say,
> "Let there be flat people," and
> there are ads and editorials.

But in the best of his poems the western great plains found the best voice they've ever had in our poetry. His fierce loyalty to the ordinary and his distaste for bluster and grandiosity were a tonic. No careful reader of poetry can encounter "The Farm on the Great Plains" and not marvel how a great poem can make a durably good poet briefly great. Half a dozen such poems in a career are enough to light a whole body of work. And Stafford's is one of those.

# Dignity from Head to Toe

Everette Maddox's poems offer themselves to a reader, any reader, with a desperate friendliness so American it seems they must have been in sales only yesterday. Today they're between jobs. The source of their manic charm is revealed in "The Poem" (from *The Everette Maddox Song Book*, 1982, hereafter referred to as *TEMSB*).

> It's a rug: jump
> on a bump and
> another humps
>
> up. It won't stay
> smooth. It's nice skin
> that keeps breaking
>
> out in boils. It's
> a cathedral, with
> every word
>
> a little gar-
> goyle. A big grin
> with all the teeth
>
> snaggled. Because
> somewhere, down deep
> inside, every-
>
> thing is not all
> right.

Only someone who loves poetry idolatrously will make fun of it the way Maddox did. The "rug/jump/bump/humps" cluster in his first stanza avidly violates good poetic taste. And why a rug? Maddox routinely proved Charles Simic's theorem that "Every cliché dreams of belonging to a great poem." This rug, too, will be pulled out from under our feet. Poetry can point to what's not at all right, but cannot change it.

In his *Rhyme's Reason: A Guide to English Verse,* John Hollander imitates Pope's "Essay on Criticism" by giving self-defining examples of each prosodic term he glosses. E.g., for dimeter:

> If she should write
> some verse tonight
> this dimeter
> will limit her

Maddox wrote "The Poem" in dimeter, a line-length widely neglected, for reasons Hollander suggests, since Skelton. On the one hand, then, Maddox's dimeter lines honor not only his debt to the tradition of English-language poetry but also assert his credentials—he can do the difficult and make it sound colloquial.

On the other hand, Maddox often wrote in strict forms, I believe, in order to remind himself that the forms are only tools for writing poems; he didn't think of himself as making order out of chaos, but as making poems.

Here are the first few lines of "The Substance of a Late Night Phone Call" (*TEMSB*):

> I have stagnated
> for 13 years
> in Tuscaloosa,
> Alabama, and want
> badly to get out.
> However, my friend
> Bob Woolf in Mobile
> tells me he has

> left a trail
> of stagnation
> all over the southeast,
> like a slug...

The first eight lines of the poem are in syllabics, mostly five syllables to a line. Then Maddox lets the pattern go. Another poem in *TEMSB*, "Breakfast" is a kind of syllabics sonnet: four tercets with three syllables in each line, and then a final couplet with two syllables per line. Why would he be so strict in "The Poem," and start strictly in "The Substance of a Late Night Phone Call" only to let his pattern tatter? Why then turn that tattered pattern back into something formal in "Breakfast"? Because Maddox wrote out of a deep ambivalence about the power and value of poetry, and such inconsistencies in his formal practice embodied that ambivalence.

> life death eternal significance
> bullshit
> from now on I'm just
> going to make little whimsical gifts

So begins "Gift" (*TEMSB*). I don't think Maddox felt that poetry was insignificant; he gave his life to it, or at least the part of his life on which alcohol didn't hold a prior lien. And what, after all, was Maddox's most characteristic rhetorical situation? Hopelessly unrequited love, pursued with a mock-courtly but crazed persistence. Especially in *American Waste* (hereafter referred to as *AW*) the role of the unobtainable was played by Suzy, who served Maddox as Laura served Petrarch.

But what else was unobtainable? Any guarantee that poetry means more than whistling past the graveyard.

I have arrived, I see, at a familiar debate topic, often proposed in Auden's famous formulation: "Poetry makes nothing happen." Yes or no?

Poetry has little or no power over the world outside the poet or reader. A beautiful poem about the destruction of trees, such as W. S. Merwin's "The Last One," doesn't still the snarl of the chain saws. Or, let's say it does, by seeping into the innermost conscious of one reader after another. Still, this process is far slower than the rate at which the trees topple, and so it makes its readers sharply aware of the speed of loss far more efficiently than it saves trees. The world blunts poetry, the way paper blunts scissors.

But poetry's interior powers are great. Poets become, I believe, their bodies of work. People like to say that, for example, Philip Levine wrote such and such a poem because he is working class and Jewish and angry. But from his recent book of autobiographical essays, *The Bread of Time*, we learn, if we'd missed it in his poems, that his working class sympathies are, in sociological terms, an act of downward mobility. Poets call this faculty the imagination. Levine has chosen to treat his anger, Jewishness and sense of sympathy with hard laborers as important, just as Elizabeth Bishop chose to treat her reticence as important, or as Robert Frost chose to treat his slyness and ferocity as important. The skeptical might say these poets chose parts of their temperaments they couldn't have got rid of for love or money, but such choices are in fact the hardest of them all. The poets chose them over and over at the desk, where poetry reigns, and where the poets made not only their bodies of work but also, and just as crucially, themselves.

Maddox chose his fate carefully, I think. Here's "Oh Man" (*AW*).

> Oh man
> I was standing
> on the corner
> rooting in my pocket
> for carfare
> & I pulled out a
> rumpled poem
> & I thought
> to nobody in
> particular
> if I could have
> wrote like this
> when I was 20
> I'd've hung out my

> cardboard sign
> on what was then
> a U.S. Highway
> & hitchhiked to
> New York
> & starved
> in grandeur

This poem is as carefully rumpled and informal as his earlier "The Poem" was carefully regular and formal.

In each case the care has been disguised a little. Maddox died in a unique situation—both homeless and widely beloved. These were not the only opposites he loved to blur: formal and informal, destitute and dignified, courtly lover and drunk with a sodden dick in trembling hand in the men's room of The Maple Leaf Bar, street poet and prosodist, Rhett Butler and Rette Maddox, et al. It's a life's work to make ambivalence a religious condition, and what will be your reward, should you do it well or ill?

> Out of print
> at God's
> Bookshop

These lines comprise one of the epigrams gathered together as "Bar Coasters" (*AW*).

Let's take a close look at "Oh Man."

> Oh man
> I was standing
> on the corner

If "The Poem" refers by metrics to Skelton and English prosody, these lines refer to the blues ("I was standin' on the corner / of Twelfth Street & Vine"), and/or to rhythm & blues. One tradition is aggressively Anglophile and white; the other is American, black and aggressively informal.

>     rooting in my
>     pocket
>     for carfare

"Rooting" is a pig's verb, although it has here an important secondary meaning: "cheering" or "hoping for." The euphemistic "carfare," which is what down-at-the-heels-gentility calls "busfare," is brilliant.

>     & I pulled out a
>     rumpled poem
>     & I thought
>     to nobody in
>     particular

We'd expect "crumpled" for that balled poem in his pocket, but here the "rumpled" part, the poem, serves for the whole, the man. Or is it the other way around? There's a subliminal rhyme between "& / I pulled out a / [rumpled] poem" and "and I pulled out a plum." *What a good boy am I?* the poem wants both to ask and not ask. Having it both ways ("nobody in particular") was one of Maddox's specialties.

>     if I could have
>     wrote like this
>     when I was 20

The answer, of course, is yes and no. At 20 he'd have not made such a blaring error for effect as "wrote." He'd have been a good boy, and he'd have wound up being rather like the aging, muddled good boy who wrote this poem.

>     I'd've hung out my

("shingle," as idiom would lead us to expect, as if the good boy were setting out to practice medicine or law)

> cardboard sign
> on what was then
> a U.S. Highway

(as opposed to the more recently built limited access interstates, often with laws against hitchhiking)

> & hitchhiked to
> New York
> & starved in
> grandeur

The implication is that by staying south, Maddox starved in, if not squalor, something less than grandeur. But his grandeur is internal and portable, and in his love of ambivalence he insisted that his grandeur be also seedy. The tone should be like the effect of the cover of *American Waste*, a title one of whose intentions is to refer to the author himself. But the cover photograph shows Maddox reading at The Maple Leaf, dressed splendidly in a three piece suit.

In "Sunrise in Montgomery" (*AW*) we learn the provenance of that suit. The title continues into the poem, the beginning of its first sentence.

> Sucks
> my heart up
> through the vest
> of my hand-me-up
> little brother's 3-piece suit
> I wore to the poultry reading—
> Walt rolls goggle-eyed
> with the post-excitements
> Bill & Momo get it on
> Ella on the tape sings
> "The very thought of you"
> Barb says "I wish I was on Baronne Street"

> But I think she says
> "I wish I owned Baronne Street"
> & I think "Me too Hon'
> we'd all be at the Fairmont
> chawing diamond corn flakes"

The Scott Fitzgerald tone (a corn flake as big as The Ritz?) here and at the end of "Oh Man" is also ambivalent. Maddox is making fun of the disease of the provinces—the sure conviction that if it happens here it can't amount to much. Grandeur, he knew, is eternal. But while he's mocking that tone, he also participates in its elegies: he know that by devoting himself to poetry, which makes so little happen except within, he had missed much. That he missed it by choice and with chivalrous mockery doesn't lessen the occasional melancholy. Here's "Cameo of Suzy" (*AW*).

> This is not a funny
>    poem
> about the life of
>    glamour & beauty
> I wanted when I was
>    young
> You weren't too late,
>    I was.
> You were the lovely
>    face
> I glimpsed in the
>    lobby
> leaving the B movie
>    of my life.

And yet Maddox arranged to leave all choice behind him, to be as quixotically and irreversibly committed as the man in any courtly love pairing. To be past the point of no return made the venture real and meant that the game was being played with real money on the table.

The editors of *American Waste* (for Maddox did not arrange the manuscript) made an intuitively fine decision to end the book with "Flowing on the Bench."

> As I was going to sleep
> on the iron bench
> on the back of the bar
> I felt all right
> I felt I was joining something
> Not the Kiwanis Club
> No
> I felt like one river joining another
> I felt like the Mississippi
> flowing into the Ohio
> Right where Jim & I
> Cairo in the fog
> Right where the book got good

# On Tony Hoagland's *Donkey Gospel*

Of the thirty-five poems in *Donkey Gospel*, nineteen have one-word titles, and six titles need only two words. One of those, "Honda Pavarotti," yokes an even more disparate pair of words than *Donkey Gospel*. Perhaps even more than he likes terse, nugget-like titles, the poet likes collisions between different dictions. One of his book's two epigraphs, from Jack Spicer, sports not only a gaudy crash between dictions, but another instance in which one of the dictions is religious:

> You ask me to sing a sad song
> How motherfucker can I sing a sad song
> when I remember Zion?

So a Hoagland reader probably should take "gospel" at least as seriously as ironically. And of course the Spicer snippet suggests the possibility that a mixed tragicomic tone may be the via sacra for this poet.

I thought of the donkey Mary rode into Bethlehem, and then—I'm not proud of this but it's true—I thought of how stereotyped Hollywood players would pitch a new film on that subject ("It's a cross between A Member of the Wedding and Mr. Ed"). But a mixture of popular culture, literature, and religious yearning simultaneously parodied and longed for is what Hoagland's adroit, moving poems provide.

Of course, there are other donkeys than Mary's, including any local ass. Hoagland has passages that require his Bottom costume, like this one:

> On earth, men celebrate their hairiness,
>
> and it is good, a way of letting life
> out of the box, uncapping the bottle

>    to let the effervescence gush
>    through the narrow, usually constricted neck.

> (from "Jet")

and this one:

>    I would estimate the distance
>    between myself and my own feelings
>    is roughly the same as the mileage
>
>    from Seattle to New York,
>    so I can lean back into the upholstered interval
>    between Muzak and lunch, . . .

> (from "Reading Moby Dick at 30,000 Feet")

The least interesting manuscripts my fellow judges and I read for the James Laughlin contest were to self-knowledge as Martha Stewart is to housework. They didn't allow doubt or stupor on airplanes or laughter at one's diligent self. They were smart. Some had got smart by subscription—they wrote theory-driven poems about desire and language, writing on the body, etc. Others knew what they felt, and with a consistent exquisiteness unknown in nature but possible, alas, in literature.

It's hard work being, and even harder work seeming, smart—the cost is eternal vigilance and we all sleep. But if you admit you're ignorant, you not only save calories but might also learn something. So Hoagland's joking professions of oafishness (e.g., see the quoted passages above) serve as clearings of the deck. And in a moment in our culture when it's apparently okay, judging by how many people do it, to make comments about "men" (not "some men") that would get you stoned if you made them about women, blacks, Jews, homosexuals, et al., Hoagland's professions of oafishness are also an ironic preemptive strike against knowing what we feel and who we're better than. Probably oafishness also stands for the important role that blunder plays in thinking. The road to music is paved with "wrong" notes.

Here Hoagland's gloomy homage to Whitman, both thanks and a spell against grandiosity:

> I sing the body like a burnt-out fuse box . . .

Another poem ends thus:

> As long as there is desire, we will not be safe.

That poem is titled "Adam and Eve," so the claim for "as long as" is huge, but these two lines that I've wrenched from separate contexts and yoked together are from the age of AIDS, which shadows a whole generation the way the bomb darkened that generation's parents.

Hoagland describes teen-age lovers whose "mission" (the title of the poem, in which the couple don't form the missionary position)

> Is to make the other blow up first.
>
> This time it's her, and her face
> takes on the troubled, *is-this-pain-*
> *or-pleasure?* look that people wear
> when the train they're waiting for
> comes through the station wall in flames,
> the long legs of the water tower break
> and desire drowns in its own destination.

Orgasm as a little death? More like a disaster movie. We walk in the shadow of death merely by having erotic lives. Hoagland is capable of quiet fury, as in these lines that begin "Benevolence":

> When my father dies and comes back as a dog,
> I already know what his favorite sound will be:

> the soft, almost inaudible gasp
> as the rubber lips of the refrigerator door
> unstick, followed by that arctic
>
> exhalation of cold air;
> then the cracking of the ice cube tray above the sink
> and the quiet ching the cubes make
> when dropped into a glass.

Or in these lines, that begin "The Replacement":

> And across the country I know
> they are replacing my brother's brain
> with the brain of a man...

But there's an underlying sweetness to these poems, and a gratitude for having survived so much human fecklessness (including, of course, one's own), and these complicate the poems' anger and puzzlement and rumple their severe surfaces. The resulting mixture has much of the complexity of a personality that willingly weathers its own perplexities and experience, rather than striking a pose of competence and trying to ride out the storm.

# LETTERS

# Peripheral Pleasures:
# The Letters of William Matthews
# to Russell Banks, Daniel Halpern & Stanley Plumly

## Introduction

I have been trying to read this snapshot of four friends as a way to talk about my father's letters. He sits on a long couch with his writing buddies Russell Banks, Daniel Halpern, and Stanley Plumly—Russ, Dan and Stan. Dan's hand is wrapped around Russ's head in a friendly, older brother gesture. Stan, caught between them, is leaning back out of the way, having thrown up his hands in mock surrender: *Do what you will!*

My father is laughing to himself as he glances behind Russ at Dan and Stan's theatrics. He holds his wine glass out of the fray. The posture of Russ's hands wrapped around his knee speaks, sotto voce, "Okay, enough of this." Only Dan looks directly at the photographer, a sly smile forming on his face.

So often for men, such teasing humor, such back-and-forth camaraderie, is really a expression of deep friendship. Comfortable with each other, with themselves and their place in the world, these men are fully enjoying the moment. Have they not shared their lives with each other for more than twenty years, through marriages, divorces, major moves, hirings and firings, and life-threatening illnesses? They know each other as well as they know anyone. Indeed, they are best friends.

―◦―

Flipping through my father's poetry oeuvre—mostly paperbacks but also a few first editions, recognizable by their tattered spines as his reading copies—I am struck by how many of the titles point to his restlessness. *Ruining the New Road*. "Moving." "Moving Again." "Driving All Night." "Leaving the Cleveland Airport." "Writer-in-Residence." "Change of Address." "The Rented House in Maine." *Foreseeable Futures*. And the list goes on.

This wanderlust—owing partly to his line of work, partly to his metabolic make-up—helps explain his particular attitude toward his literary friendships and, by extension, his correspondence within them. My father surrounded himself with the things he loved—books, music, wine, art—not only because they were the totems of his habits but also because they served as the ritual tools of his art-making. They made him up as they propped him up; they were extensions of his body—his past, his family, his inescapable foibles; they were his emotional life contained in static animation. So, it's not surprising that he shared these brotherly loves with his "brothers," and that just this bequeathing love is on display in these letters.

With a poet as self-conscious, skilled, and controlled (controlling?) as my father—equally known for his erudition and his wit—what are we to expect from his letters? Perhaps the same wry evasion we find in his poems, posing as manners while allowing him yards of aesthetic distance? Or maybe a stripping of conceit to reveal bald revelation? Maybe a little bit of each? (If he could have his way, I am sure there would be no published correspondence at all. Read the poems, he'd say, if you want the story.)

As I went through the letters, I came across more of the sporting banter crowding the above-mentioned photograph. On the surface there is the conviviality of sports talk, wine notes, jazz and opera news, and travel anecdotes. (All of these men have traveled widely and have found great pleasure in their excursions.) There is also much in the letters about the writing life they shared and about their careers in the academic world, much said about the intimacies of family life and marriage.

Often my father threads serious discussion of his emotions into his small talk, though pain is muted or avoided altogether. In the opening letter in this selection, for instance, after talking honestly about his relationship to women, he moves quickly into a discussion of his broader social life on the University of Colorado campus. The conversation then goes immediately into baseball banter—the knee-jerk nature of rooting against enemy teams. Then, beautifully, this half-formed idea morphs into the realm of politics, culminating with an emotionally charged jibe at Richard Nixon. The familiarity of friends—much like the address of poet to reader, perhaps—spurs my father into eloquence.

But the action is not all freewheeling all the time. There are moments in the letters when my father is startlingly honest, candid, self-revealing. Here, he is writing to Russ about his last thoughts on his depression and subsequent therapy:

> It's a dreary business, and it and related problems have finally led me to the psychiatry I scorned so loudly and suggestively for so long. The process itself doesn't interest even old friends, so breathe easily. On the other hand, you & I have been too long out of touch, and this is part of the central matters that have occupied my life since you and I were last keeping each other abreast of our lives, so of course I think to mention it.

Throughout the letters, my father talks of hardships, worry, and his own deep-set insecurity. But he's always pulling back, always restrained by a refined decorum. I'm fascinated to see my father write in different voices to each of the three friends, matching his tone and subjects accordingly. But openness, warmness, humor, and honesty permeate them all the same.

In compiling this selection, I wanted to show something of my father's "swing" as well as the power of understatement in his correspondence with friends: how talk of wine, hoops, and the po biz not only stands in for real emotion but also carries it; how this kind of talk works as gesture; and how gesture works as a kind of physical force. Voice as love, or something like that.

~

One night, halfway through a bottle of ripasso, I stumbled upon an old record of my father's: a rendition of Bach cello suites played on a baroque cello—one of those three-album boxed sets with a picture of the soloist on the cover. The ancient, pint-sized cello crouches between Anner Bylsma's knees. Bylsma's shirt collar has a distinctly 1970s flair, and his hair is a ruffled mess. His wrists are cocked, fingers precise, in place.

As I listened to the opening prelude (Ali and I had it played at our wedding) and sipped at the earthy wine, I absentmindedly glanced through the box. I came across a sticky note attached to one of the album sleeves, a note scrawled in my father's crabbed handwriting: "The record of Suites 3 & 4 is in bad shape, but #1, 2, 5, 6 are fine." It took a while to realize that the note was meant for his sons and that, when he wrote it, my father had been imagining a day in the future when he would be gone. "They're wonderful music," the note went on, "both lean and rich. It's music you listen to alone, and only share with people, those few, you really love." I sat in the dark and sipped, listening as carefully as I could to the music that made me both happy and sad, alone and not alone.

*Sebastian Matthews*

1974 – 1978

2 January 1974

Dear Russ,

A long & pleasant Christmas break here, with my parents & Susan visiting for a week of it. The boys love that kind of company and the profusion of gifts it means for them. My parents & Sharon get along well, which is nice. We had a postcard snow the day before Christmas. A genial & silly holiday. I'm glad to be back down to 4 in the house, so I can get some work done and live by a daily routine more nearly of my own dictatorial making.

The boys say you took them to Boston for a Celtics game: what a treat for them. Thanks. I'll have taken them to see the Nuggets once, where the offense looks like a Celtics game, lots of running & fast breaks. The ABA doesn't play defense so well, though, and the Nuggets are terrors for playing slightly better than playground defense.

I'm playing ball for a local bookstore, Brillig Works, and enjoying it. I played enough tennis this summer & fall to be in fairly good shape and it's a pleasure to stay in shape through the winter, rather than puff up the habitual ten pounds, like a bladderfish.

The Follain ms. is at New Directions & Atheneum now, and we'll see if anyone at either locale is overwhelmed enough to forget his or her good commercial sense. The book can only pay its way if published in paperback, allowed to stay in print 5 or 6 years, selling by word of mouth, occasionally getting a sales boost when used in class by some enthusiast.

There should be copies of your books about to appear, right? I'll be eager to see them, love to you all

Bill

# 11 January 1974

Russ,

I hope it's a good vacation there & in Fla., full of ease & slow days & escape from vacation when that gets necessary.

Two big storms here, but no effect to me. I'm working on Lillabulero matters & trying to sort out the job situation, and falling lava would hardly effect my daily deliberations, though I'd dress differently for my walks.

Ai writes she's sick, miserable in her job and has no new poems (will send them if...) so we'll not count on her for the last issue. Fred Busch's agent sent a good story, free to us, which I've written back accepting. And I heard from Steve Katz; he & I have taken out the first small piece from the series he sent us, and one other late in the series which he might be able to peddle along with the first one, and we'll print the rest, in order, in the last issue. I've got some poems from Jim Seay I'm looking through, and will have a choice by the time you're back.

On the job front, polite demurrals from everywhere. I think the Emerson job may well be a trap, a mismatch between the School's personality and mine, and am hoping to turn up as many alternatives as I can before time comes to decide. A small program like Emerson depends on perpetual care: Jim & Charlotte Lindgren are always there, don't want time off, have both invested in their jobs more of their psyches than I'd want to invest in any job. They don't apply for grants, hope for sabbaticals, imagine saving money to take time off—all things I'd want to do, and want to be able to leave a job behind without feeling it would rust in my absence. Also they depend on personal loyalty, institutional loyalty: if one teaches there regularly, rather than a one-year basis, one puts out a lot to the program, and enters a web of loyalties & obligations.

Bob & Nancy Morgan & Benjamin spent a good day here; I wish it had been longer. Bob's book is fine, though perhaps a little early: there are a few too many Son of Red Owl poems in it. The "Climbing" sequence is cut about 40% from the version I gave you, and far better; a similar ruthless attention to whole ms. would benefit it, and in fact the script I would have would still be nearly long enough, lacking only 3 or 4 poems, if he did that. I'm reading it with an eye to such suggestions, and will pass it along when you get back. He sends greetings, and wishes he'd been able to intersect.

I've got a couple good poems on the back burner, as they say in the Globe sports columns, but here's a good one, done.

Love, Bill

# 8 August 1974

Dear Russ,

Good times now. 3 weeks until moving, with some possibility I can move some things up in advance. The boys are very settled into their routines here, and I too. I'm teaching only writing courses (2) in the fall. Tuesdays & Thursday, so no preparation to speak of. I'll be glad to unpack everything, have my whole study spread out and everything out of boxes. Still getting lots of work done, but wouldn't want to work in this skeletal way for very long: it's more like trying to work on the road than at home.

I'm occasionally seeing tennis opponents. Reg Saner, some local hippie carpenters who will work on the house. But much of my time is either by myself or with the boys. I find I enjoy celibacy: the women who've made an effort to flirt I resented, recognizing emotionally what I've noticed abstractly: flirtation is a form of emptiness (used as a physics & descriptive rather than moral & condemnatory word). Something wants. It is a complicated kind of imposition, but an imposition, and it invites the person on the receiving end to make impositions on himself. I haven't much missed other forms of social life this summer: the boys are here after all, and I've had visitors. An entirely different rhythm in the fall, I'm sure, and I'll be geographically set up in such a way that it will be a project to have a social life above a casual one. Interesting to see what forms I'll imagine for that.

Looks as if Rose, Morgan, Bench & Perez are the best 4/9 imaginable of a modern ball team, but fall short of being 9/9. Dodgers seem to have it; maybe the Red Sox will survive their division, and then Oakland, so I'd have some team to root against the Dodgers for.

On the other hand, or cheek, Nixon is in increasingly exact touch with his own petard, and that gives me a deep vengeful pleasure.

Love to all there, Bill

2 April 1975

Dear Stan,

Thanks for the vita, which I've sown in Xerox. Now for the rounds, like early rounds in the playoffs: poet vs. prose director, male vs. female, making a decision vs. acting like a provincial university, and all the subtle creases in between that make up university action.

Life moves slower here than if I were God, a good thing for the universe. All those tax reports in, air angel . . . I think I'll have something definite to report in 10 days or 2 weeks. What makes us think we can hold off decisions that long I don't know, but we are going to do it, procedures and all, I can tell.

Heavy snow the last three days, on top of an earlier unmelted pelt of eleven inches. Snow up to my asshole. Also snow so dry at this altitude & in crisp, almost crystalline air, that it seems like science-fiction snow, on a planet whose chemistry is based on silicon, or inert gases.

Playing pick-up games of basketball twice a week or so. I'm a little better when I haven't boogied all night, but not enough better to justify any fantasies of amazing grace.

Love to you & Hope, Bill

12 July 1976

Dear Stan,

Sickened unto death by summer school, I'm distracting myself by working on the house, soliciting material for Iowa Review, doing a little writing. Sharon's been doing a little indoor painting and fussing. I get the good jobs: garage, septic tank, etc. Paneling downstairs has been ripped down; some walls will be painted and some covered with rough-cut cedar. Bathroom floors, now in a lovely vomitorium-pattern linoleum, will get done over in ceramic tiles. Nothing like owning a house for a second career.

I'm going at the ms., final flurry of precisions, now. I think I'll junk the "& selected" part, since these new poems are a fairly dramatic (even though organically developed) growth from the last book, and the retrospective format might obscure that. No way to guess how Peter Davison may react to that—probably he won't be happy. Settled on *Sleeping on the Ocean* for a title. I'll send along a Xerox by this week's end.

Bought myself some stereo equipment (new receiver and new turntable; a tape deck is coming up (a stuck key temporarily provided this interesting typo: ape deck)), and naturally some new records, mostly Lester Young re-releases, to play on it. Good fun. What a consumer I can be when I get going! I understand why we want to be rich, and why we shouldn't be.

Bill

20 September 1976

Dear Stan & Hope,

Reg Saner wrote me a note that warmed & chilled me (take that John Crowe Ransom), so clear a mirror did it seem. I hadn't seen him much before I left Boulder. He said he's missed me, which might sound odd since he had a miser's habit with affection, as if it drew interest by not being expressed.

 I seem to have done the same when we parted in Iowa City, and I hate the thought that I made you feel you'd done something to offend. For one thing, I love you two too much to be offended, or if offended, not to let it go. And second, you'd done nothing of the sort. It was me, about whom the following things were true at the time:

 1) Enthusiasm

 2) New place, new situation with the boys, lot of the WASPily repressed anxiety about those & other newnesses

 3) Reunion with Sharon after a hard summer for us (nothing melodramatic, but enough to make meeting again vibrate)

 4) My hatred of sentimental goodbyes (which can banish sentiment from goodbyes if allowed free reign of censorship: when I left on the train to prep school my mother shook my hand. Then, Father says, wept like a cloud for two days, once I was dryly launched)

Actually it depressed me to see you go, as I'd have loved it to be around you longer, or all year. You're the best things about Iowa City and the minute I get here you leave.

 Anyhow, that's all there is to it, and I send my love.

 Next letter I can tell you the saga of Richard Murphy & Richard Murphy, a marriage made in Taiwan.

Love, Bill

## 27 December 1977 / St. Martin's

Dan—

Life's not bad here. We're right on the beach. There's tennis nearby, cheap rum, the usual inducements. This island is staggeringly beautiful. We're on a strip of land between the sea and a lagoon, on the French side. Snapper & langouste in all the restaurants. Last night we grilled some fish the maid brought us. Fantastic. What are they, we asked. Oh, she said breezily, that's a red one, and that's a striped one, and that one, that one's a Bullhead. Bullhead!? They were all delicious.

Yrs, Bill

4 July 1978


Dear Dan

Thanks again. I had a good trip, despite everyone's preoccupations & glooms. What the hell. I have my own.

Mary Feeney & I are getting the Follain manuscript that will be out in the fall into shape. Besides the prose poems, Follain has two other important prose works: *Canisy* (a book about F's home-village) and a tiny book on the introduction of the potato to French agriculture & cuisine (this little book is essay-length, and Mary & I will translate it by mail over the summer; I'll send you a copy when we're done). Follain's widow has just sent us the name of the bibliographer who has worked on Follain. It turns out the the guy's wife has translated *Canisy*. I'm going to ask him if he'll send me a copy. If she's done a good job, I'll send it to Antaeus; if not, I'll send it back. A long shot, but somebody should do it well.

Do you know any of Follain's prose? Very different (and I think better) from the wonderful poems, which you must know from Bill Merwin's translations.

Got your eating notes from France (Do you know Liebling's *Memoirs of a Feeder in France*?) I'm sending a copy to my father, since he & I plan an eating binge in Paris, fall 1979, before we take Bill & Sebastian on the canal trip.

Mail sent to me c/o the dept. here will get forwarded to the various spas I'll haunt this summer. Keep in touch. I'll have some wine notes shortly.

Yrs, Bill

1978–1981

21 May 1978

Dear Stan,

That piece in *APR* is a wonder, and the only thing I've seen in print or heard recently that seems better is the batch of new poems you read in Oxford. The work you've done the last 2-3 years and the ways you've made it seep into and infuse your writing is wonderful, and the work you're doing now and will be able to continue to do—that's the real reward, after all—is and will be the stuff to live by.

That first. Second, how pleased I am to be read so intelligently & generously. It seems both just & praising, and that's a rare reading, indeed.

Found this in an old French magazine, a quote from Follain: "... dans les champs de son enfance éternelle/ le poète se promène qui ne veut rien oublier."

It's probably prose, but the way it's set up on the page I can't tell, so just in case I've preserved the line break.

Just back from Montana & Utah. Saw Dick Hugo in Missoula. He had a can of worms in the fridge and looked to have reclaimed Montana the instant he crossed its border. He has a drink now & then, I'm sorry to report. Otherwise he's fine. Jim Welch, William Pitt Root, Tess Gallagher & others. In Utah Dave Smith and some others. Dave in excellent form, rather more settled than I've seen him ever. We watched the 6th game of the Nuggets series, in which my heroes looked like a group of tall Pakistanis given 48 minutes to find the many interesting differences between this new game and field hockey.

Love to you both, Bill

16 August 1978

Dear Stan,

Finally, Seattle. The city is wonderful, and the house (though it needs plenty of work, and a nearly liquid supply of dollars just now, when I want some floors sanded down, some painting done, etc.). I'll not rouse the dept. much until I've been here another week and can get some settling in done.

The boys arrive the 26th. Dick Hugo will be in town in a couple of days, and he & I will hit some baseball games together (the Red Sox will be in town). It's not a major league town, it's an American League town, but that's better than Boulder offered.

I'm plenty tired from my summer, though the monies I gathered will help with settling-in expenses and I'm glad for them. A number of interesting literary projects afloat (one: I've been asked to contribute an essay to a collection of them on Nabokov, and want to write something about his English poems), and as soon as I can get the moving chaos stilled I'll be happy to be working at them, tireless as Richard Howard.

I'm itchy to re-enter literary life, and will re-enter it with mixed feelings: I'm itchy to be at work, but I liked a little spell as a civilian, an ordinary rather than a special monster.

Write or call, amigo,
    Yrs, Bill

## 5 June 1980

Dear Russ,

Jim Dickey is in town, to have a hiatal hernia operation performed by a local doctor who invented the latest important innovation in that procedure; he's come through the operation healthy & feisty. At Dave Wagoner's urging I went over to see him; recuperation is boring and he wants visitors, an audience, company, all these. He's not the demon he seemed years ago (though neither are we the demons we seemed to ourselves years ago). He is charming—those thuds you hear are birds falling out of the trees. He's not without smarm, self-aggrandizement, etc. either. Tells great stories. The best one, which requires a thick and self-parodying Southern accent, is actually a routine from Jarrell's *Poetry & The Age*, about a young poet praised for grace and wit and charm, who might be tempted by this definition of himself to repeat it endlessly. "He's like those Southern girls who come north, and are told—whatever you do, don't lose that charming Southern accent—and in two months they sound like Amos n Andy."

The quarter here has ended, and I'm trying to take care of the many details necessary to leave town for two months, and waiting to see if folks at Murray will pull it out at the last minute or, as I hope, not.

Getting things done is complicated by the fact that I've been on the edge of one of my little fugues of inertia & withdrawal (remember the boxes I never mailed from Ithaca), a pattern of temptation all too familiar by now and which I'm trying to learn to handle by never repeating a mistake such as those I used in dealing with it last time, and in recognizing as early as possible the ways I pretend at first that I'm simply over-worked and under-caught-up, rather than veering off toward familiar wilderness. I'll have skirted the edge of this one with fewer people hurt & puzzled than the last one, and less reluctance on my part to come out of it and pass through the short period of shame between it and normal life.

It's a dreary business, and it and related problems have finally led me to the psychiatry I scorned so loudly and suggestively for so long. The process itself doesn't interest even old friends, so breathe easily. On the other hand, you & I have been too long out of touch, and this is part of the central matters that have occupied my life since you and I were last keeping each other abreast of our lives, so of course I think to mention it.

Around here there's a Beringer 1975 "Santa Barbara Wine" for about $4.25 a bottle; it's 99% Chardonnay and 1% Reisling, and would pass muster at twice the price. It will be good for another year, and if you can find any of the Martignetti's or elsewhere, snap up some, white wine costing what it does since it became the national hip aperitif.

Love to you all there, Bill

17 June 1980

Dear Dan,

I don't know when there will be enough "Farron Ridge" to send it out of state. It's the new "jug wine" ($5.00 for 1.5 liter magnum) from St. Michelle, a white. Red will follow this fall. It's all Chenin Blanc, Chardonnay & Reisling, and they've promised to blend the best available wine each batch, rather than strive to duplicate a recognizable house style or taste. It's terrific; it's the closest thing to a cheap drinkable white wine I've had in several years, and especially since the "glass of white wine please" phrase replaced "Perrier, por favor." Pale gold in color, slight spritz, just enough glycerine to "coat the spoon," though it doesn't have legs in the Betty Gable sense. The under-taste, or structure, is the Chardonnay; on top you get the Chenin Blanc & Reisling.

It will not restore the poor to joy—nothing in our economic life can do that, at this stage of the game, when every time an Emir sneezes sperm counts in Washington & London fall—but it is a gift to the down-at-the-heels gentility of this life, such as it is.

Yrs, Bill

## 24 October 1980

Dear Russ,

I've just finished the last details for the second edition of the Follain translations, out in January. We're adding some poems, revising a few tiny points in the translations, correcting one horrendous typo ("I couldn't write one of them," says an old lady of her children: she should say "raise"). Madame Follain has sent some goodies over to make the book special—photos, drawings, holograph pages, etc. And this time the pages will be numbered. This is the same press that did Charlie's new version of White.

Otherwise, lots of writing & reading.

The basketball season seems hard to predict or understand, this early, though. For the fun of it, I hereby announce a Milwaukee-Philadelphia final, with Milwaukee winning in six. The Sonics seem waterlogged and unorganized, neither of these characteristics being usual to a Lenny Wilkens team. The season is still more fun in the papers than on the floor, though I'll probably get to the Phoenix game tomorrow night, my first of the season. Phoenix still hasn't solved its rebounding problems, now has two big guards who like to hold the ball (Davis, moved from forward, and DJ), and Truck Robinson & DJ don't get along. LA looks terrific but has only eight players and can't get through a whole year without injuries two years in a row. The Sonics will jell by the playoffs, after early muddles, but not enough to stop either LA or Milwaukee, who should be the league surprise if Lanier stays healthy.

Do you know what day you & I are supposed to read together? I'm reading at Hampshire College on the 24th, and am ready now to fill in the other dates for that jaunt, in February.... Sharon is a galley slave for UW, teaching three courses a quarter and treated, the way big schools do their instructors, like a useful rat. Absence from academic life has made her heart grow fonder for it; by spring she may well loathe it. Only 10% of the teaching jobs in the country carry any dignity or ease with them, but since academics persist snobbily in treating themselves like members of a gentlepersons' club, they have to coo over cheese parings as if they were Brie. It's not that we produced "too many PhD's" in the last two decades. We churned out just enough hungry and unemployed folks to replace the disillusioned as they drop off the lumpy gravy train. Actually it's the teaching writers, who prefer to think of themselves as the Israelites in the desert, who've prospered most during all this.

Yrs, Bill

19 April 1981

Dear Dan,

Drank a bottle of the 79 Acacia tonight, the top of the three lines (Napa Valley-Carneros District/Winery Lake Vineyards). Kistler also makes one from Winery Lake Vineyards, a place I'll try to learn something about this coming weekend, which I'll spend in the Napa Valley. Going to do a reading at Cody's Bookstore in Berkeley, and then one at UC-Berkeley, though in a night school class, or something not very official. Anyhow, they got bucks, and the excursion to the Napa Valley thereby gets underwritten.

    Also drank with Stan & Jim Welch & Lois & Deborah & Sharon two bottles of Clos du Val 1978 Merlot. If you're ever going to love a California Merlot, this is the one. Tastes like a Pomerol. Finegan's wine newsletter had raved about it, so I tried it—it's fat softness, without the burnt aftertaste so many California Merlots have. Try one, anyhow, and see what you think.

    The Acacia is not quite up to the Kistler, but is very fine.

    Jim Ulmer says he knows where some bottles of Kistler are, and I'm going out tomorrow to see what I can buy. I'll split with you whatever they've got.

Yrs, The Zinfandel Kid

1982–1988

## 5 August 1982

Dear Dan,

Bill's in Amsterdam, Sebastian's at his mother's for the summer, but otherwise the world seems crazy. While the Cincinnati Reds have just lost their 8th game in a row, a team called the Seattle Mariners is six games over .500 and three games out of first place. Something very sinister has happened to our sense of order and tradition. I went to watch the Mariners beat the Yankees 5-4 last night, before 42,900 folk, and the only disappointment was that George Steinbrenner didn't have a heart attack and topple from the skyboxes, growing visibly purpler as he plummeted, with the TV cameras lapping it all onto videotape so that a grateful nation could watch it over and over, and it could be played between innings on the giant scoreboard screens without which no new stadium is complete nor old stadium renovated.

On the other hand, between Houston and Seattle I have seen five ball games this season, and none of them outdoors, so I'm clearly contributing to the collapse of Western Civ myself. In fact, it's my major summer project. I'm writing, reading, and doing as little of redeeming social importance as possible. I make tapes for the deck in the new car (a 5-speed, 4-door Honda, a very solid and stylish little car), I cook outdoors on my deck with that smug look males get charring meat on their own property, and now and then pull a cork or two.

Hope you are thriving. Give Jeannie my love.

Bill

## 21 December 1983

Dear Stan,

All's well here. I'm off to NewAwlens on Friday, and will be back here the 3rd of January. I told Dan—but by the time you get this letter you'll know all this—where you'll be when you get in, and I assume you & he will have found a way to get together for New Year's Eve.

John Ashbery is ill and is taking a leave for the spring, and through a kind word from Dan the folks at Brooklyn College are offering me a slot for the spring. I've taken it, and if some version of Memphis State doesn't happen to this one, I'll teach in Brooklyn Monday & Tuesday every week and make about $16,000 for the spring. This could be a foothold job, too, but in any case it's welcome.

The apartment is wonderful, in its way, as you'll see in February. Russ called the other night with news that a particularly good & cheap red wine is available at $39.00 a case from a wine store at 79th & 3rd, and I have two cases to pick up in the morning. My mother is here, but I desert her at appropriate intervals and go uptown and stay with Arlene. Have been to see the De Kooning show at the Whitney, a stunner, and went w/Russ & Kathy to hear Betty Carter sing at Fat Tuesday's the other night (I'd never heard her live.) Tomorrow evening I will go to the party for Bill Merwin & bride Paula. NY life. There's also the parking & the dirt, and, just now, the early & fierce cold, but it's fine.

Love, Bill

19 March 1986

Dear Stan,

I'm off to Michigan tomorrow for a quick raid—2 readings in a day and a half—and then back, and then I'll actually be here for a while.

Finished work on the book. Now I need time to type a fair copy of the manuscript and get it off to Peter Davison, to find out if I'm to be a Houghton Mifflin author or not. Maybe this coming weekend, when, so far, the only thing on the schedule is to go to see Susan dance Saturday night and have a late dinner with her after the performance.

Brooklyn College conducted a series of interviews (with me, with CK Williams, with half a dozen other worthies) for someone to replace John Ashbery, for now a series of one-year contracts and eventually full-time. At the last minute Allen Ginsberg had his agent call them, showed up for an interview (from which, according to Jon Baumbach, the committee emerged with the looks of women who had just experienced their first orgasm), and will be offered the job. But I'll be on duty at City next fall.

When are you coming through NYC?

Yrs, Bill

## 15 February 1987

Dear Russ,

I've spent much of the weekend reading in preparation for a short essay on Tony Hecht's use of Horace as a tonal example, and anything else interesting to myself about Horace and uses of the classics. This for a feature Syd Lea is doing on Hecht for *New England Review*, which I agreed to contribute to if I could have this topic I devised for myself.

I did take time out to watch the Lakers-Celtics game today, a good one. Should be a great finals this year. If Magic remains this forceful, the Lakers might win it in 6 or 7. Mychal Thompson is going to help that team a great deal.

Dan's back from California, where they seem to want him but half time. He called the minute he got off the plane and pretty straightforwardly opined as he won't take it, sounding wistful not so much for that job but to have a different set of problems in his life, I expect. One big liability Dan mentioned for the job I'm glad he saw so clearly: it's a straight English Dept. job and those are academics. It wouldn't all be like teaching at The New School or Columbia. Dan's never really had to work with academics but may sense intuitively how quickly he'd attract their jealousy and insecurities.

Bill

# 3 March 1987

Dear Russ,

A busy week. Last night I introduced Gerry Stern and Garrett Hongo at the Y, after a weekend spent getting ready for Barry Taylor's visit. Spent an afternoon with Daniel Lang, looking at new pieces he'd done and preparing to select a painting by him for the cover of my next book, which already has a title (*Mood Indigo*) and some beginning pages. There's a PSA board meeting this week, and there are, as always, letters of recommendation to write (deadline for Bread Loaf recs is coming up) and various time-eating chores & kindnesses to perform for students and young writers. I make a grumpy Mother Theresa.

The 13th we're flying down to spend a long weekend with my grandmother, who's been lobbying for a visit and whom I haven't seen for a while except in the midst of all the birthday flurry last summer in Cincinnati. Back the 17th in the evening. Then the 19th I'm off to Chattanooga and the spring swirl begins in earnest.

My grandmother can be exhausting company. She's a non-stop talker, rather like a baseball announcer during a rain delay, and she's plenty willful. She's also old and lonely and I'm very fond of her, so it's time to go down and get our metabolisms trampled. The secret is to go in pairs, so one can listen and the other can be on the beach.

There are other diversions down there, including spring training and a restaurant in Tampa with a mammoth and interesting wine list. One day we'll be there the Reds and Mets will play an exhibition game.

You probably have seen Bob Morgan by the time you get this. I've had a couple of notes from him recently without much news (he's lonely as can be up there) but saying how charged up he was for you to be there.

Love, Bill

25 July, 1988

Dear Dan,

I'm delighted that *Antaeus* wants "39,000 Feet." Seems to me that my poem "An Airline Breakfast" appeared in *Antaeus*, too.

 A brief report on a week in Sicily: very hot, dull food (except for the seafood pastas & specialties at Jonico, in Siracusa, and you have to insist that you're not a tourist and that you want their best). Sicilian wines dull. Archeologically, a great excursion—the Greeks & Romans left some wonders here and the Sicilians have been too poor to ruin or exploit them wrongly.

 A good second level hotel in Rome: La Residenza, Via Emilia, 3. In Milan, this one [Hotel Manin]. A good place to eat in Verona: the restaurant in the Due Torre. Better than 12 Apostles. *L'Arche* was *chiuso per ferie*, alas. I had a terrific meal at Gaultiero Marchesi in Milan. He's a megalomaniac and some of that stains the whole operation, but only until the food comes. I drank a La Pergole Torte, a wine you'll remember from that tasting dinner at Union Square Café. I've had it thrice now and it never pales.

 Stable mates here have included Rita Dove & Fred. Now they're gone, but Molly Peacock's just arrived, because her boyfriend, Marc Consoli (Sicilian born and an interesting composer), has won a month here. Then a clatch of hitstorians, social scientists, and social engineers: the *specialite* of the Rockefeller *maison*. Among them, briefly, was Paul Sigmind, professor of politics at Princeton; his wife may be the mayor there? She wears an eye patch and has one color-coordinated to each outfit she wears.

 It's not been hot here as in NC, but it's been hot. I play tennis in the early morning on a rather beautiful court the Rockies have thoughtfully installed atop the peninsula, and manipulate the shutters and windows in my bedroom and study like a regular little Mediterranean. Every 4-5 days a lurid, spectacular electrical storm surges through the lakes and clears out the heat and haze that have been building, and then you can see to Switzerland in one direction and damn near to the Dolomites in another.

The food here isn't lavish, but it's tasteful and stylish, as are the wines. While we're at dinner a maid comes to turn down the bed, but the Rockies are too damn tasteful to put a Hershey's Kiss on the pillow.

Yrs, Bill

1990-1997

9 May 1990

Dear Dan & Jeannie,

Drue was just to the castle for a hit & run visit from London, and that brought out the cloth napkins.

I'm off this weekend to spend a couple days with Mother in Newcastle and to escape the castle's sturdy cooking (the fare the night Drue was here was, according to the menu, "cauliflower cheese" and tomorrow night the "veg," as of course everyone says, is "mushy peas') for two nights.

But in fact the castle is quite homey and the staff are as nice and kindly as can be, even while enduring the "heat wave" (it shot up to 82°) we had last week. The castle is on a latitude with Moscow and northern Saskatchewan, and the heat had them dropping like flies, as the local doc said when he came out to treat the cook.

I'm off to Edinburgh this afternoon. This format is wonderful for getting reading and writing done, but it is also capable, for me, of provoking savage flashbacks to prep school, and thus sets a high value on off-campus forays.

So I'm off to the Scottish National Gallery to look at some paintings and the Royal Mile to look in the shop windows. There ought to be a wine shop in the city that can top the selection available in Bonnyrigg, the nearby ex-colliery town and commercial center for the castle.

I trust my trusted and rusty Honda is holding its own against the winds and deer urine, and that you two are thriving.

Love, Bill

20 August 1990

Dear Dan,

When we got here, sunset was 8:20 pm; now it's 8:00. The news about fall is clear.

Still, we have excursions to Siena and Urbino unmade, and another buying spree at the Enoteca in Perugia. And we're both working steadily in the mornings, which are of a nearly pristine character when there's no mail, no phone machine, none of the gabble of usual daily life. I'm working on translations from Martial as well as on poems. I wrote one tiny essay, on brevity and epigrams, in the Adirondaks, but otherwise I'm leaving prose, for the summer, in the cobbled hands of prose writers. Including, of course, my wife, who's at steady work on what looks, more and more as the pages pile up, like a novel.

There's a rackety tractor here clearly closely related to the one in Polgeto. Everyone's plowing now—time to get in the winter wheat to keep the country in pasta—and the owner of this antique likes to plow at night.

Love to you & Jeannie, Bill

## 26 September 1992

Dear Stan,

We'll meet at the Rick Jackson Pro-Am if not before. Both of my assistants from Bread Loaf (I had a third, Jean Nordstrom but she was assistant staff, and the other two more my junior, as so many people are these days), James Harms and Laura Kasischke, will be there—both good folks.

I'm off Friday to inspect my grandchild, in Seattle. Bill named him Raven, showing a flare of his mother's genetic contribution.

Gramps: Coo.
Raven: Caw.

Then back Monday, to teach that night at NYU—I finally gave in to Galway's & Sharon's persistence. Tuesday night, Falstaff, Verdi's last opera, written at 80! At the Met. If the right bass has the title role, it can be splendor. Boito, Verdi's librettist (who basically sweet-talked Verdi into writing his last two operas, Otello and Falstaff, when Verdi was half-ready to live out his last days being called Maestro whenever he went in Milano), has translated much of the insult-flurrying and badinage of Merry Wives into very lively Italian, and it has a real Shakespearean tone, for all the Italian open vowels, which make the curses and flyghtings all rhyme. Bardolpho's famously huge and red nose, for example, combined with Falstaff's sense of how much sack he's paid for to make it livid, produces a little phrase about the thirty years Falstaff has watered that purple fungus. All of this wordplay at high speed, and much of it buried in quintets and sextets where all the singers are singing different texts at the same time.

And then Wednesday I fly to Ann Arbor to read and spend two days with Sebastian and his MFA classmates there.

Come to the city one of these days. 15 November, a Sunday night, Charlie Williams will be here and I've offered to cook dinner and put a lively table together (Galway maybe? You?). But come whenever you call.

Love, Bill

16 May 1995

Dear Russ,

*Rule of the Bone* provided many pleasures, including watching over your shoulder and as you squared some accounts, personal and artistic both, that didn't quite settle to zero at the end of *The Book of Jamaica*. It was good to meet the shadow/arrow lyric, which has never left me all these years, again. I like the Hitchcockean cameo appearance of you & Chase. But these are insider jokes. I don't mean in the "reference of Ted Berrigan" style, for some of these pleasures are available to your regular readers—insiders themselves, as they should be.

More important is how good a book it is—your best meditation yet on race, I think, and my favorite, now, among your books for excellence of the prose. One can hear Twain, the tutelary spirit of the book, and more faintly Sherwood Anderson and Elmore Leonard, and here and there a whiff of a less dotty Hawthorne than NH ever managed to be. You started out—I'm thinking of you first visit to Bread Loaf—in the story-teller rather than the stylist camp, but one of the pleasures of reading your work these many years has been to see you become a stylist on your terms—a fine act of instinctively self-knowledgeable truculence.

I like the way the Jah stick and the Uzi get positioned on opposite ends of a bar graph about violence, control & technology.

It's a wonderfully smart book without ever insisting to its readers that they admire it for being smart it's as if, instead, the book simply assumed it had to be smart about its story to tell it well.

I'll be in Andover MA for Sebastian's wedding over the Memorial Day weekend, and then in Paris 4-13 June and in Bloomington IN 23-30 June. Otherwise I'll be here, the cottage industry equivalent of a dark, Satanic mill. When are you two headed north, in the midst of all the publicity for your book?

Do you remember the name of that hotel in Mexico City with the long lobby-like bar trisected by indoor greenery?

Yrs, Bill

28 July 1997

Dear Stan,

The standard of poetry reviewing is lower than I ever remember it, and at the highest I remember it, it didn't challenge flood stage.

So I thought David Baker's piece in the recent Poetry was very good on your book, a little too respectful on Bob Hass but not dumb, good on Sharon Olds, a little by-the-numbers on Steve Dunn and a dream review for Linda Gregerson.

Prague was fun but I had to sing for my supper. But supper was $2,000 and an apartment for a week just off Old Town Square. So what if the Czech national vegetable is pork? The cook birds well; we ate chickens and ducks. There was time for seafood in Venice. Spider crabs, scampi, sardines in sweet & sour sauce, cuttlefish, etc. Plus a sensational sea bass in a wild fennel sauce. We spent an afternoon finding Tintoretto's house. We walked and walked, of course—no cars in Venice and the bus is a boat. We spent a lot of time on the water, having brought week-long vaporetto passes when we got off the train from Prague.

I've finished my "translation" of *Prometheus Bound*. It's possible my shot glass of Greek is more than my heavy-hitter predecessors (Lowell, Heaney) can claim, but of course it's the result in English that matters. I think both of their versions are slightly clotted and literary, and actually playable on stage, though it would have to be directed like a Monteverdi opera. I bring less brilliance to the table unless an increase in clarity counts as brilliance.

Love to you & Judith both, Bill

29 July 1997

Dear Russ,

Celia & I are back from a happy jaunt—a week in Prague and one in Venice. CK Williams & Catherine are putting in a brief appearance, too, at the Prague Summer Writers Workshop, but our stints didn't overlap.

My Selected Poems in Hebrew is about two months away. The publisher is launching a series of books of poetry translation with an initial release of four books, by William Blake, Octavio Paz, Wyswlwa Szymorski and me, the Where's Waldo? of the list.

There's a limited edition (100 copies) coming out any day from a fine press with Bucknell. *Night Life*—it's a cross-section of nocturnal pieces from my various books. It's interesting to put such a book together though perhaps the work is lost on fine printing collectors who are not readers so much as squirrels, their cheeks puffed out with fine editions of John Updike poems.

I'm hoping the Hebrew book will occasion a trip to Israel, which I'd like very much to see.

But for now I'm at home, with the air conditioners and office gadgets plugged in and the meter running. Peter Davison is hoping to get a new manuscript from me by mid-September or so, and I'm in the process of handling the book (like kneading dough, some) to see if it feels whole or still unfinished and fragmentary. If it's ready it would come out in the fall of 1998, and if not it would probably get delayed a year.

I love Venice because the bus puts you on the water, and because the whole paranoid what-defensive-site-could-be-better-than-the-middle-of-a-lagoon idea has got turned inside out into great picturesque romanticism. All the Tintorettos and Titians and Bellinis don't hurt, and of course the complete absence of cars is the future the rest of the planet won't be able to find. A rainy day in Venice during which you walk and ride the vaporetti and gape at painting and walks some more is a memorable wonder. To visit La Fenice, the Venice opera house some electrician torched because his work was so far behind schedule he was facing severe contractual penalties, is to think very harsh thoughts about money & humans. I hope they feed the bastard to the scampi.

Love to you both, Bill

# INTERVIEWS

# Living by the Long River:
# Excerpts from Interviews—Early, Middle & Late

### From "Moose Interview"

CC: Mr. Matthews, you were born in Cincinnati. Did you spend most of your early life there?

WM: Not really. It was always a center; that was where my father's family was from. I was born in wartime, so spent some of my early life in Cincinnati while my father was in the Navy. Later we lived there, but only three of those years was I at home except on school vacations.

CC: Did you have what might be called a literary upbringing?

WM: Ours was a house with books in it—books that got taken off the shelves. My mother read to us when my sister and I were young. On car trips there would be readings from Thurber, from Ambrose Bierce. But literate would be a better word than literary. Books were associated with pleasure. My mother taught me to read before I went to school, so when I got there and found that reading was supposed to be work, I figured I was beating the system.

CC: I've noticed that some poets maintain that they have a sense of themselves as poets very early, that from childhood, almost, they wanted to write or to be poets...

WM: Not me. Everybody in a family will tell you a different story about your childhood, as you are probably aware. My mother claims that she knew early what I was going to do but I think that's hindsight. I don't believe the story although I like it; I think it's her way of saying she is pleased by what I do. I grew up wanting to be a range of things, from a professional basketball player to a psychiatrist.

CC: Did you want a literary career by the time you went off to college?

WM: I didn't know what I hoped to do. I suppose I guessed, in an unconscious way, that I'd wind up teaching English. A good guess, as it turns out. On one level it's a way of getting paid for reading, beating the system, just like in first grade.

CC: How did you finally start writing?

WM: I wrote poetry from the beginning, though what I read most avidly in those days, my early twenties, was fiction. Some poets like the idea that writing poetry is a priestly activity, somehow the highest of the arts. It's nice to think well of your job. But can one finish a book by Proust or Nabokov, let's say, and think the creation of such books in any way secondary to poetry? Fiction writers invent huge worlds; they don't count on a wonderful metaphor in line four to stand, somehow, for the entire Eastern Hemisphere. But my skills, I must have sense, are a poet's, not a novelist's. I think, though, that my great heroes have always been prose writers.

CC: Many poets, when first beginning, had certain poetic heroes after whom they tended to model themselves, like art students learning to paint from the Masters; were there people like that who especially influenced you?

WM: I've had a series of such people. My earliest literary hero was not a poet; it was Nabokov. I admired his interest in memory as a creative faculty, and his incredible precision of effects. He seems to me now, of all the great novelists, the one most interested in how the whole mind works. There's no mental activity he can't make physical. But his work is full of the physical world, too. He can describe—I can't think just now of a greater ability in a writer—what it feels like to be alert and what you notice when you are alert.

When it comes to picking poetic heroes, it's difficult; at different stages of your life you have different heroes. You don't usually begin with Keats or Stevens. They are too big. They overwhelm you. A likely hero for a beginning writer is someone who's very good in the generation immediately preceding. I found James Wright an important poet to me. He was an Ohioan and wrote like an angel. Later on, Roethke. It would be hard to imagine anytime in the future when I wouldn't think Stevens a hero, but at first I didn't want to mess with him. I didn't understand the poems well enough. I didn't understand how much was at stake in them, how deeply personal they were, and they scared me. Williams, of course. And there's a kind of clarity, a focus in Elizabeth Bishop's work that's really interesting to me, that I've never failed to love and find useful. One may reach a stage—I'm not sure about this—where he doesn't stop learning, to be sure, but where he isn't any longer an apprentice writer, and the people he's used as models and heroes become only poets (only!) again. What fun it will be to read them then.

CC: Do you have a favorite story about a poet that you've known? Like taking a leak with TS Eliot or something?

WM: What an anecdote that would make, like a recording of light rain in Seattle. No talk. All atmosphere. It sounds like an early poem by Eliot, both reticent and daring. I wish I could tell it, but I never met him.

Auden came to an undergraduate class I took from John Hollander on the history of the lyric poem. It started with Pindar and was supposed to arrive at the present, after two semesters, but we only got into the early nineteenth century. Auden was editing the Yale Younger Poets Series in those days, and had come to New Haven to be at the ceremony announcing that year's winner. Hollander sometimes missed a class, so when he was a little late we were restive: how long should we wait before leaving, etc. I loved that class and favored waiting long. Then they came in. Auden talked about the songs in Shakespeare's plays, and then afterwards a few of us students were allowed to tag along for some drinks. I had a dull glimmer that day how poetry stayed alive: here was a poet of great importance, who had been a rebellious young literary figure and who was now passing into literary sainthood, talking both about great poetry of the past and about the first book he had chosen for the Yale Series. I saw how much poetry he had got by heart, as we say, and how it was all a long river to him, inside him even. And how he lived by it. I was a junior in college, and until that day I'd thought that my interest in poetry—a rather ignorant interest, but a real and passionate one—was weird, somehow peripheral to what I ought to be, like the way I loved basketball and cared about it "too much." I began that day to sense there couldn't be too much. I even came to feel that way later about basketball, and about whatever I loved.

# From "A Conversation With William Matthews,"
## *The Black Warrior Review*

MARCEL SMITH: What kind of manuscript volume did you handle [with Lillabulero]?

WILLIAM MATTHEWS: Well, at the beginning we were happy to get 15 or 20 manuscripts a week. But after we left Chapel Hill, we had, in addition to whatever following we had built up there, two other regional constituencies, because Russ Banks was in New Hampshire and I was in Ithaca. At that point there were times when it would be 50 or 60 batches a week. That was at my box in Ithaca, which was the central mailing address, but some of the stuff—maybe 15 or 20 manuscripts a week—went to New Hampshire, too. And we would be sending them back and forth, so it was really killing for a while.

MS: That kind of volume puts an enormous burden on editors and that must have something to do with how you look at what you get. When you're reading through batches of poems, how do you work?

WM: Well, what you wind up doing is developing shorthand methods. It's always dispiriting for people who submit poems to magazines to hear how editors do that. It sounds terribly cynical to them, but it really isn't. The biggest problem in reading a whole bunch at once is to save your intelligence for the ones that are really worthy so that you haven't fried your brains by the time you get to the good ones. So what we would do, I would go through fast to weed stuff out, and then try to get to the good ones before my brain had turned to cotton. When we started, there were four or five of us around the magazine with very loose lines of power and then eventually it got down to two. I thought it was easier the fewer editors we had. At the beginning we needed other people because neither of us knew anything. I had not read any of, say, James Wright's poetry. I had discovered John Haines' *Winter News* in a bookstore in Chapel Hill, and that was a great event to me—an event similar to what discovering Robert Frost must have been for people. I don't think

Haines is as great a poet as Frost, but it was the same event in language to see that something could be that clean and that clear and colloquial. So we were learning as we went along. At the beginning having four or five to argue everything out slowly with was really educational. I was learning much faster from that than I was from any formal study. But once Russ and I learned a little bit and started getting our personal bearings as editors, it was better to just go on and not have other people to be concerned with.

MS: Did you ever formulate anything like an editorial policy about what sort of thing you were looking for, or did you just rely on your own sense of what was good?

WM: No, we didn't have a policy as such. Banks and I were lucky that we got along as well as we did. We are still close friends. And our tastes were different enough that we balanced each other. In some ways our editorial policy would look like one of these New Math graphs where you have a little almond-shaped overlap area. That was what we wound up taking. He was more attracted than I am to what you might call the objectivist tradition in American writing, and I was more interested in a meditative and more subjective kind of work, so that a certain amount of interplay and argument and agreement between us was what we wound up printing.

MS: It strikes me that if you have two good editors, that is a very healthy way for things to go.

WM: It was frustrating at times for each of us. For example, I've always liked Peter Wild's work. Peter sends poems quickly to new magazines because he writes so many good ones and wants to get them placed. I can remember when they first came in I thought, This guy is really good. But it took Russ a while to get interested enough to agree with me. The same thing happened the other way several times and it would be frustrating because one of us would find somebody and it would take the other person two or three batches of submissions to get acclimated enough to finally give in.

MS: You also printed some interesting things through the Lillabulero Press. How did you get into that?

WM: We sort of drifted into that. We wanted to do some broadsides and we had a press. We leased it through the University YMCA. We used to go up there at seven in the morning in this little office on the second floor—about the only time of day it was cool for about half the year there—and we would like to work early in the morning or late in the afternoon because once the press got going it got pretty close in there. This thing would handle 8 ½ by 14 sheets and we thought, That will make a nice broadside. And then we realized we could do pamphlets by printing on that size sheets and folding them in half. So we did one or two pamphlets just by local writers. And then a guy named Robert Peterson, a poet from San Francisco, came through whose work each of us began to like. He had had two books published by Kayak Press and he had a new book and wanted someone else to do it. He had a great loyalty to Kayak, but I think he didn't want to be a house poet. So he came through to give a reading and said I wish somebody would publish these poems. That seemed like an open door to us, and so, rashly, we went through it. He'd seen issues of the magazine, you know, and a little bit of what we could do, and he was kind enough to say to these two people he had never heard of that had this little press, Sure, go ahead and publish it, and so we did. A lot of the stuff we wound up doing worked that way. There was a young guy there who was a terrific poet named Robert Morgan who had some very good poems and they seemed to have no place to go so we wound up doing a book of his.

MS: How many titles did you do in all?

WM: We did three full-scale books and about 19 pamphlets by the time we were done.

MS: How about the pamphleteers? How many of those went on to bigger and better things after you printed them?

WM: Several. Wild, for whom we did two pamphlets, now has a publisher in Doubleday, and his second book followed rapidly on the heels of his first. Morgan went on the get a publisher and so did a couple of other people. We did some translations that Charles Simic had done, and we did some Robert Bly translations. These are people who had their publishing ties already made but who had a small group of things that they didn't want to blow up into a whole book. And so we did them.

MS: This whole publication thing is a fascinating nightmare. I mean the relation between what gets printed and what lasts. Take the competitions, for example, like at Yale and Pittsburgh. What percentage of the Yale poets, for instance, have gone on to do anything anybody paid any attention to after they have won the prize?

WM: To look at the list around 1901 or whenever it was is really depressing. It's like looking at old baseball cards when you think of all this talent and energy that has somehow fizzled. That's really an interesting question, that whole problem. Say when you're my age, around 30, there are 15, 20, 30, 40 interesting poets around, but in another ten years there'll be only eight or ten. And whatever the sorting out principle is, it's obviously not talent, because all those people are talented to be noticed in the first place. It must be some kind of endurance or persistence or some kind of power to continue.

MS: Might there not be some kind of correlation between endurance and creative power? A person can have a certain kind of sensitivity to language and a sense of how to get words on the page and write say one good book. But to write two or three you have to have something more than just talent to draw on. You've got to have materials.

WM: I think that could be. If you do have the sensitivity to language and the willingness to work at the poems until they're good enough, you can out of the conditions of youth write one or two books. There is a kind of wonderful loose ends untied energy in good first books that is recognizable at a certain stage in life. But then as you push on, the question is whether you can invent or imagine a life for yourself. At that point the poems come out as very different kinds of poems.

MS: It strikes me that this has some bearing upon Keats' crack about Wordsworth being the poet of the egotistical sublime, explaining why in his view Wordsworth had burned out early: because Wordsworth was writing not only about his own life in a very narrow way and he used up his capital and didn't have anything else to draw on. A great many enormously talented poets in our own time have written out of their guts in a way, and many of them burn out early, maybe for that reason.

WM: I think describing one's own life in poems is risky. The imagination will pick representative or extravagant moments and life doesn't throw those moments up fast enough, and so unless you develop a kind of crash life to go along with the work, you run out of stuff. In other words, you sin more in order to gain grace.

MS: John Berryman, for instance, seems very consciously to have done that. In one of the interviews that he granted shortly before he died, he was talking about the enormous suffering he had undergone. I forget exactly how he put it but it was something to the effect that he imposed the suffering on himself—keeping himself in a condition of torment in order to have materials to write from. Dylan Thomas, I think, must have done the same kind of thing. There must be a better way to do it than that.

WM: Maybe what matters is the relationship between your poems and your life. If you handle it right, the poems in some way could invent the life. That seems to be a possible antidote to suicidal self-absorption. Even a poet whose thematic range seems as narrow as, say, Mark Strand's does can turn out to be extraordinarily fecund because in some ways his poems are about the invention of the self and the disappearance of the invented self and the problems that causes. That seems to provide him with material to travel with. Mark is always moving along in a way that would get a poet with a more confessional or biographical bent in trouble. I don't know, this is pure speculation, but maybe the high incidence of conventionally extravagant crises in writers' lives—divorce, alcohol, and so forth—has something to do with a deep fear that they're going to run out of material. The fear of drying up is certainly real. I've never known a writer who didn't at some point say MY GOD, maybe I've spent it all! So that if you have that fear, stasis and calm and the terms of a kind of mature adult life in some ways become your enemy.

# From "Talking About Poetry: An Interview with William Matthews," *The Ohio Review*—Stanley Plumly & Wayne Dodd

OHIO REVIEW: Do you have a stance—in either confronting your own poetry as you write it, or looking at somebody else's—that you want the poem to essentially take risks, risk a kind of disaster, invite chaos?

WILLIAM MATTHEWS: I think so. I'm a believer in the notion that one of the functions of art should be to disarrange patterns of certainty in the psyche, that, really, the psyche is very conservative. I've never understood the tremendous force behind it, and why the acceptance of the notion that art organizes, and that the world is a kind of intolerable chaos, and that if it weren't for the comforting, organizing ability of art we would somehow be in an awful situation. It seems to me that the great nightmare of 20th-century life, particularly, is a life that's organized all too well, and that what we really need is to have our certainties shaken up badly. There's a famous book by Morse Peckham, called *Man's Rage for Chaos*, which is very polemical and so forth, but I respond to the general drift of it very well. (Susan Sontag says at some point, "the purpose of art is to make us nervous." That's a little understated. You can imagine her coming home, you know, and saying, "Gee, I just saw King Lear and it's a terrific play, it gave me a migraine." I mean, I wish she hadn't used the word "nervous;" that seems so much an urban intellectual's word.) Maybe the purpose of art is to make us temporarily inconsolable and lost and wild. But the idea that it should give us this tremendous comfort I've never understood. And so I have a prejudice, I'm sure, in favor of a kind of art which does take risks. I think it's much more fun to write so that you feel you're not repeating yourself, and you don't know what you're doing. That's more fun than the feeling that you're going through the same motions which have already become too familiar to you. But also as a reader I like to read things which cause me to be places I haven't been before, and I much prefer that to an art which has a too-orderly quality about it. I'm sure this is one of the reasons why it's never occurred to me to write in traditional verse forms. I imagine if one wrote in them for a long period of time you would find some perfectly fascinating technical problems would come up. But I'm so much a believer in the notion of surprising yourself, and taking risks and preferring disorder to order, that it would be almost temperamentally impossible for me to do it. I see the whole notion of chaos anyway (in that phrase "order out of chaos") as very strange. I mean, you wonder what these people imagined chaos to be. Mostly they're people who get up every morning at eight o'clock, teach an Aesthetic Theory class at ten, get the department mail at twelve o'clock, give a graduate student exam in the afternoon, go home and have two drinks before dinner. That man's definition of chaos is not a very trustworthy one, you know.

OR: True, but that's what I was taught to think and believe.

WM: If we're talking to André Malraux during the period of his life when he's fighting in China, then perhaps if he says "All this chaos" . . . There's a kind of chaos which is awful—the moment before civilizations collapse, or when three members of your immediate family or friends are killed. There are kinds of chaos which are awful, and there's a lot of apocalyptic fervor in the air, which is saying, suddenly, "If all this blood would flow, everything would be OK." That notion bothers me enormously. I don't want to be in the position of exhorting blood to flow. But I think that in terms of dealing with our ways of seeing things and our way of reacting to disorder in art and in the world, the notion that what we should immediately do is organize "chaos" and not have those emotions is very false and stultifying.

OR: The history of this planet, the history of our whole animal life, is this chaos you're speaking of, this accident, this chance, this random sampling. That's where the energy is.

WM: Yes, that's right. I was thinking exactly of energy. I was thinking of Blake, of course, energy being eternal delight, and so forth. I use the metaphor of evolution a lot, and it seems to me to be the place where . . . it's the force which makes things, which causes things to happen. It's extraordinarily painful. Everybody hates change, even those of us who talk about risk all the time, and love to talk about risk and energy and so forth. There's a side of us which is resistant to change.

OR: You used the word *evolution*. I perceive in a poet like Simic, even in a poet as apparently cerebral and civilized as Mark Strand, and certainly Bly and Wright and Stafford, a kind of allegiance to the primitive or pristine or primary.

WM: There's a kind of atavism in this. Charlie Simic has it strongest: "Maybe it's soon someday we'll be going through deep snow raping widows"—"Whoever swings an ax has grown fur." That's not right. But there are lines like that which suggest that we might have this awful plunge backwards. I have this odd theory about that. In a lot of poets that all seem to have been born in 1926 or 1927 (except for Stafford), their particular myth is the myth of the journey. There's a sense of a need to set out on psychic journeys. Galway Kinnell has this. You certainly feel it in Snyder and Ginsberg. They're myths of progress in a way. There's a sense that we'll undertake some spiritually difficult and very exacting travel of one kind, whether it's an interior journey or whether it's a cultural one, or whether it's an actual, isolate one as in Kinnell and Merwin.

OR: Do you mean a kind of Whitman open road?

WM: I think perhaps it's the open road. Simpson's fascinated with the idea from another point of view, coming out through Whitman primarily. I don't sense that in the younger poets. Strand, it seems to me, is the location of the change. In Strand's poems people are always moving, but nobody goes anywhere.

OR: Stasis.

WM: Yeah. You get this excruciating sense of stasis and also a rejection of certain myths of progress. His poems are often described in terms of stasis, and narcissism, some kind of awful locked combat with the self, and so forth. But there's another side of it which is maybe less negative, could be less negatively described: it's a rejection of these myths of progress, it's a world which is lithocentric. The stones don't move around much; they just sort of sit there in the desert, and the wind goes over them, and the sun comes out, and they get rained on, and that seems to be the way their life works. Maybe a very typical poem for our generation would be a poem which starts out proposing a context in which something ought to happen, and the assertion of the poem is that it's not going to. We'll be here tomorrow. We'll get up and we'll eat. And we'll survive the day. And we won't go. There'll be no footprints on the glacier. We won't climb into a bear skin. And whatever those deep rituals are (which are journey rituals for an older generation of poets), we'll have to invent other ones. I think atavism is one of them. And sullen survival is another. I love Charlie's poems about it because the primitive life to which he's reverting is full of bloodshed and danger. It's not a bunch of groovy savages in touch with nature, it's . . .

OR: Frightening?

WM: Very frightening. And they are in touch with nature in some ways, the people in those poems, but they're also in touch with the menace and violence and aggression of nature. And I believe them. It's not as Bly said about Wright (making one of the few negative comments he does in the essay on Wright in The Sixties), that even the ants are well read. You feel that all those people in Charlie's poems, those huns and nomads wandering around, are not terribly well read. They may be in touch with the landscape in certain ways that we aren't, and this might be good, just in the way that, in fact, we know the American Indians were. But there's also a tremendous amount of violence. And that's important to note.

OR: That certainly isn't a pastoral sense of what the natural world is.

WM: Yes. And Charlie fought through that. I mean his first book, *What the Grass Says*, has some very over-prettified pastoral poems in it, in which they describe a nature in which there is no death, and so therefore not a very believable nature, because it seems to me that death is the fuel of nature. And that's what I like about atavistic poems: that sense gets in.

# From "Interview with James Duffy"

JAMES DUFFY: How did you get started writing poetry?

WILLIAM MATTHEWS: Every honest answer to that question should begin the same way: "I started reading it." Nobody is likely to become a poet who didn't start reading poetry early on and didn't stop. When you begin to read poetry, I suppose we could say, you are in danger of becoming a poet.

There's a crucial next step. You tell yourself you are going to try to teach yourself to write poems very well, and even as you make this step you realize how mad a notion it is—like a poor child setting out to become a great polo player.

Still, in those days I was not about to declare myself as a serious poet-to-be. Later in I was in graduate school and not happy with the prospect of a lifetime doing scholarly work. I needed to make some choices and that's when I started writing seriously. Even then I was careful to present to the world a sort of amateur status.

JD: Why were you careful to do that?

WM: Why would anyone not be careful in undertaking something for which he has no credentials and no way to prove to himself or others that this commitment is likely to bear fruit, which has no economic or other visible utility, and which guarantees a considerable measure of failure (some of it publicly visible) for the first years of doing it? Not to be careful would be a little nuts.

I take that care to be ordinary, by the way. In truth, few parents look at their new baby through the glass wall of the maternity ward and hope for an avant-garde child. They hope for a child who will blend in with the others and be a little luckier and fare a little better.

A lifetime writing poetry is not necessarily a happy fate, and I think most beginners have ways to ward off, with one set of superstitions or another, just such a gloomy premonition. One way is to buy several black turtlenecks and lead a lobster on a leash. Another is to cover the fire of one's passion and fear.

JD: Could you say something more about that fear?

WM: Poems, even very early ones, have the power to engage the poet's emotional life. They're like little prayers to a very powerful household god.

One of the things you realize when you set out to teach yourself to write poems is that the difference between your own baby efforts and the great poems you love is huge, and that you have no idea how to get from one place anywhere near the other. You fear you've set out to do something impossible, and that your inevitable harvest will be failure and sorrow.

The beginning of a writer's life is a peculiar time, because you need to treat your own talent very seriously before you even know if you have one. It requires a sort of faith a little different from the brashest egotism. And this happens at an age when you are not usually—I certainly wasn't—emotionally flexible.

JD: How did you become interested in jazz?

WM: Luckily for me, I didn't grow up in one of those houses where the thing to do about the larger world was to keep it away from your kids. My parents had books, records, curiosities. They saw to it I got piano and clarinet lessons.

In my fantasy life, I wanted to be a white Lester Young. But I was not good enough, or willing to work hard enough.

JD: But jazz has influenced the poetry you write.

WM: There are things about phrasing and rhythm and tone I've probably learned at least as much from listening to music as from reading poetry.

In musical improvisation, you're thinking and feeling your way as you go, and that becomes part of the rhythm of what you play. There's the larger rhythm of the time signature, of course; let's say it's 4/4. But the rhythm of each phrase is made partly from the process by which you got from the beginning to the end of it. If you spend a considerable part of your adult life listening to Billie Holiday sing or Tommy Flanagan play the piano, you learn something about the possibilities for the kinds of rhythm in poetry that can't be measured by metrical notation, but are closely allied to the question of "phrasing" in jazz, the small surges and dawdles that are part of the process of discovery and become to a considerable extent the rhythm of what's been discovered.

JD: Your poem, "Fellow Oddballs," from your book, *Foreseeable Futures*, seems to illustrate what you are saying. I'm thinking, in particular, of the third stanza:

> and here's to us on whose ironic bodies news clothes
> pucker that clung like shrink wrap to the mannequins.
> and here's to the threadbare charm of your self-pity.

These first two lines almost leave the reader breathless. It's very similar to an improvisation—the language is stretching as if it were musical. And then there's the moody undertone of the third line, which is also a place to pause and gather your breath . . .

WM: For most of the way through the first of these lines, through the word "bodies," or so I imagine, the reader has no idea where this odd toast is headed. Then there's a dip in diction from "ironic bodies" to "shrink wrap," and then the clothing imagery leads us through "threadbare" to, perhaps, a fresh way of thinking about self-pity, or at least one that reminds us that it is not the emotion itself that is reviled, but letting anybody notice us in the grips of the emotion. That turns out to be why, the passage discovers, it was so interested in clothing and packaging. Part of the tone of the passage, to my ear, is a pleased self-amusement in the speaker's voice that he's not quite sure, himself, what he'll say next. Much of Thelonious Monk's work is driven by a like engine. I'm not making a comparison in the quality of the resulting work, mind you, but in procedure.

An utterance always has the potential to be quite different by its end than it suspected when it started out. The extreme and dazzling example of this in our poetry is Ashbery's work, in which almost nothing stands still for long.

Perhaps Ashbery achieves such effects by simply not going on good behavior when he composes, but letting his mind doodle and play as it does when he's not at the desk. Part of the accuracy obligation I take on in writing poems is not to make the language in my poems any less complex than it is in my head when I'm not writing but just being usually alert.

JD: Your poetry lingers rather lovingly on the complexities of everyday existence. A poet whom you admire for a similar interest is Horace.

WM: Horace has written a great poem inviting a friend to dinner (Epistles I, 5). At the center of his imagination are things left out almost entirely from many a body of poetic work: friendship, pleasure, talk, food—much of what actually sustains us. For Horace, these subjects were not small, and he expended on them no less skill than Virgil needed to write his great epic.

JD: In his poems, he's often at dinner, in the Forum, in the marketplace, fascinated by his fellow humans' behavior.

WM: Likewise, there's an interesting assumption about the audience in Horace's poems. "Now if you ask me, what is it, Horace, you're driving at, here is my answer," he'll write. There's a powerful fiction of conversation between equals in those poems.

It sounds familiar to those of us in the Whitman line, as all American poets are: you invent an audience and speak to it—"Alone with America," in Richard Howard's tolling phrase.

But of course Horace had a patron. He had had in fact the patron, Maecenas. Augustus read Horace's poems and found jokes in them. He could have written as if from an inner circle with no pretense. But his stance was inclusive, convivial, democratic. I suspect he was capable of deep depression, and that may have accounted some for Horace's invention of his audience of friendly equals, an adult version of a child's imaginary friend.

JD: Why did you choose to include your translations of Martial in your Selected Poems?

WM: I like them and hope readers will too. For some it may provide and introduction to Martial.

I've always loved Martial's poems, and thought I heard a tone in them that hadn't been translated quite right. "Elegant nastiness" might come close to it. And the best of his epigrams have a terrific emotional and moral accuracy to them; they're very passionate poems.

I started translating them when I had accepted an invitation to a writer's retreat in Scotland. I'd work on my poems in the morning hard and then be done with that intense attention for the day. It was lunchtime, then it was after lunch and I was surrounded by wet sheep and made a serious prey to boredom. I'd brought Martial texts with me to work on with just that problem in mind.

In any case, the classics should be translated every generation or so. That's how I read them, in various translations from various periods. Thus the Martial we come to know is in some useful way the sum of his translators, and those translators aren't in competition with each other.

JD: Speaking of collaboration, could you describe the procedure you used for your translations of the Bulgarians?

WM: Well, I have no Bulgarian. William Meredith and Richard Harteis were editing an anthology in which American poets, picked without regard for their knowledge of Bulgarian (and almost none of us has any), made versions from literal translations provided by folks whose Bulgarian was very good indeed, but who had no skill at writing poetry in American English.

Purists hate this procedure, but neither the Bulgarian nor the American poets involved hated it or the results. And readers who would otherwise have to wait for purists to leave off hating and take on the job of translating the poems "right" were pleased to have some view of what Bulgarian poetry is like these days. If we made errors, others can correct them. Translation, even by this admittedly approximate method, is collaborative.

Also, I liked very much having the Bulgarian poems on my desk. I worked on them while I worked on my own poems. When I got stuck in one, I'd turn to the other, and when I returned I often got unstuck quite easily.

JD: Your poem, "Mingus in Diaspora," from *Time & Money*, seems to me to address many of the issues of writing poetry we have discussed today. Could you elaborate on that?

WM: The great jazz bassist (and great composer) Charlie Mingus was someone I heard perform frequently. He was immense and volatile, a terrifying figure, particularly to the pianists he fired frequently, sometimes in mid-set. Probably because he composed at the piano, he had very exact ideas about what his pianists should and shouldn't do.

His passion and perfectionism appealed to me, and his small bands in the sixties seemed to me the best that jazz then had to offer.

His music has mattered to me for thirty-five years, and now that he's dead, the poem looks around, so to speak, to think out loud what of his fierce spirit has survived, and how someone might make a music so durably fascinating—by what sense of history and time, by what effort, by what stubbornness. There are two poems in the same book about Mingus performing—anecdotal pieces that are, I hope, larger than mere anecdote in their implications. How is it that we make, if we can, beautiful things?

# From "Blackbird Interview with David Wohan & James Harms"

DW: Why don't we talk about your first book, and your early work? Those poems seem very rooted in some of the period styles of the sixties and seventies, the short imagistic poems of Merwin and Wright, Bly, sometimes... who you've written about in your essays. How did you get attracted to that sort of writing, that Deep Image writing that was in the fashion then?

WM: Yale also didn't administer courses in very recent poetry. You went further into the modern era than Oxford and Cambridge did. In those days they taught nothing after 1900, I believe. At Yale you didn't go much past 1945 or so. I didn't really have much idea of what was out there. I started buying books and reading stuff that other people around me were reading. I had never read Roethke's essay, "How to Write Like Somebody Else." It took me about two years to get to reading Roethke in any form. If I had, I might have figured out that it would be interesting to systematically imitate somebody. But what I did was I wound up imitating the Zeitgeist, in a way. I wrote in a period style. And it had one advantage for me, the prevailing short, heavily metaphorical poems. The short was the biggest advantage. Because when you're trying to teach yourself how to write, one of the things you want to do is go on. If you're working in a form that allows you to go on until you make a terrible blunder, and the possibility that you are already pretty close to the end of the poem by that point, it's happened. They were short because it was what I could manage. It takes a while to teach yourself how to get a poem, how to keep a poem going. I wrote these very short poems which you could say of that kind of poem that it begins and it starts to end almost simultaneously. I thought I could make something the structural integrity of which would hold up if it were comparatively small, and that if I did enough of that I could learn to go on longer. So, I think the short was probably a very important part of the attraction for me. I have a metaphorical imagination, or bent, had one just as a speaker, as a kid before I ever wrote things down. And so the idea that the making of metaphors as a kind of thought had occurred to me in some natural and untheoretical way at a fairly early age, and so I thought, "This doesn't feel dauntingly difficult," I thought. It was more difficult than I first thought, but it was something I could do.

JH: In terms of starting with those early models, do you feel as though you were part of something very quickly, part of a period movement that you identified with?

WM: Well, yes and no. I identified . . . I liked James Wright's poems a lot for reasons I didn't understand at the time. I liked Merwin's poems a great deal. It took me a while to realize that one of the things that was interesting to me about them is that they were poems by somebody who was rather learned and well educated who had figured out a way to write without wearing that. Two of the poets who are about my own age whom I ran into first, one by geographical accident was Robert Morgan, was living in Raleigh in those years and used to come over to Chapel Hill a lot. And I was sent Charles Simic's first book and actually reviewed it for what was nearly, probably the third or fourth issue of Lillabulero. And I felt attracted to some things in both their work a lot, but I didn't feel a part of a movement in any large sense, and I didn't have the same enemies. In fact, I was too naïve literarily to have any enemies. I wasn't reacting to anything except probably unconsciously reacting to a rather Augustan undergraduate experience in the Yale English department.

On the other hand, I was very grateful for that. The English exam that you took there to qualify for an honors degree was a sit-down exam. You sat down and wrote an essay, here was the question, there was one question. They gave us five different translations into English of the same passage from the *Odyssey*, and the question was "Date the translation; give your reasons for the date. Name the translator, if you know or have a good guess. Finish each of the five sections of your essay by describing any recognizable features of the way the verse is operating that belong to a particular period of literary history." And I had an education well enough that you could answer that. And I never, never regretted it, always been very grateful for it. But if you're starting out to write, you have to turn your back on some of that stuff for a while because issues of decorum, and issues that could pretty well be identified by reading a copy of *Understanding Poetry* rather closely are not helpful to a young poet trying to teach himself how to write. That education was hardly an enemy, but it wasn't going to be useful to me until I had done some stuff of my own during a period when I ignored it and pretended with middling success that I didn't know those things.

DW: I'm just thinking, when you bring up Merwin and Wright, and thinking of how the interest in those short, subjective, surrealist poems, also starts to manifest itself in your work and the interest in the epigram. Horace was Wright's favorite poet, and I know he's one of yours.

WM: Always. And there're a couple, I can think of a couple of poets, not contemporaries, who interested me a great deal as a reader when I was that age but whom I didn't know how to make any use of in terms of writing poems. I'm thinking especially of Auden and Byron, with both of whom I came to feel some temperamental rhyme as a reader very early, but I didn't know enough. I didn't know enough literature, I didn't know enough about how to write to make any particular use of them. It was like reading Stevens at that age. I thought, "I know this guy is terrific, but I don't understand these poems yet, so I am going to turn my back on it for a while and come back to it when I have a better chance of figuring out what I can do here." It also allowed me to put some of that stuff aside on a kind of "to-do-later, when-you're-grown-up" shelf. I found it a very useful model to the extent that poems in that tradition, this is less true of Merwin—it seems to me than some of the other poets—are almost never about a social world. That seems to me a defect of those poems. That didn't mean I wouldn't use the style to help teach myself some rudimentary things about learning how to write, but it always seemed to me that the way in which they took place in an unpeopled landscape was a problem for me, whose imagination is more social in a number of ways than some of those poets were.

JH: I think the period style that you used seemed to have run its course pretty quickly, though, in terms of finding a different voice. It seems like around the third book, *Rising and Falling*, the poems change quite a bit. What were you conscious of at that time?

WM: I don't know how much it was conscious, but a lot of what seems to be aesthetic decisions, particularly if you take a narrative interest in your own life or career, are really made on a much more inarticulate level than that. For me a major thing that happens is that I get bored. You write a certain number of poems that have certain things in common and after a while you've begun to solve whatever the problems that you could elicit from that style, or that form, or whatever, that body of subject matter. You get to the point where you really begin to know pretty well what you are doing. As I near that point I get bored, and I get eager to get stupid again and to take on something I don't know how to do yet. I think some of it was a fairly subliminal sense of that.

Also there was subject matter that I was interested in writing about. A lot of the sort of imagist/Deep Image poems were about the assumption that subject matter was a stand-in for something else. In that sense, they're sort of Freudian, there's a latent and a manifest content, though I think Jung may be the presiding theoretician to those poems rather than Freud. But there's still that sense that the poem is the vehicle to get at something which is unspoken or unspeakable behind that. That's in fact not the way I think of poems. I think of poems as having engagements with subject matter which produces something that isn't subject matter and that really is poetry. For me, at least, I need to have it in order to write.

Andy Warhol once invited Mingus to come out to East Hampton to discuss making a film. Mingus had written the score for Cassavettes's movie *Shadows*, and it was a big hit among the hip. So he went out to East Hampton, and he kept saying, "Well, what are we going to do?" And Warhol said, "Well, we're going to improvise." After about a day of this, Mingus turned and went off in a huff. And he could go off in quite a huff, given his size and authority. And he says, "You can't improvise on nothing, man."

For me, in some sense, subject matters are like chord changes; they are not what poems are about but there's something about subject matter, as there is about memorizing the chord changes to a really beautiful song, that allows you to get to the thing which isn't subject matter in poetry, which is a transmutation. But it's not about something that's not said. It's finally about that thing that you make out of the chord changes or out of the subject matter. And so in that sense, those engagements with subject matter were very important and the way those Imagist poems seem to be, on some level, queasy about having subject matter and treating the subject matter as a kind of distraction, the way Language poets think of certain kinds of plot as a kind of the opiate of the masses, which you have to get rid of in order to find out what's really going on. For me it's never the point, but it's always been the vehicle.

# From an interview with Rachel Levine (1996)

RACHEL LEVINE: What do you think is the role of poets and poetry in the U.S., or in the world?

WILLIAM MATTHEWS: Poetry keeps the unofficial history of what it was like to be human in a particular period of time. It takes our emotional lives seriously. Official history—who made war on whom, who signed what treaties, etc.—is so large, even grandiose, in its perspective, that it can barely notice individuals, and that category includes us all.

I think another function of poets is to keep the language clean, and to get off it as much of the dirt that advertising and contract writing and other coercive forms form of language promote. Some dirt is good for language, though; an absolutely clean and antiseptic language would be a dull one. But too much dirt and you can't see the mushroom. And so some proper proportion between the two is sought by poetry.

I don't what other claims should be made for poetry. There's a long tradition of saying that poets are the unacknowledged legislators of mankind—a dreadful assignment. If nominated I will not run. If elected I will not serve.

I feel perfectly comfortable thinking that because poetry is very important to me it's worth pursuing. I somewhat lament that poetry doesn't carry a bit more respect, but that seems to me the culture's loss rather than the poetry's, finally. One of the things poetry had better get used to is being undervalued. And it may be better to be undervalued than to be overvalued. Think how hard it was to be a poet in the Iron Curtain countries, where the power of the good word was taken so seriously by the dictators that you could get killed or jailed for just doing your job as a writer, which is to basically not to call a spade a garden implement. So perhaps it's healthier to individual writers to have poetry be a little undervalued. It was maybe better for the art, to be treated very seriously, but it put some of the practitioners of the art at great risk.

RL: So what's your take on the performance, spoken word, slam poetry that's happening?

WM: Well, it's not what I do, but that doesn't mean it's not lively and interesting on its own. I'm in favor of people amusing themselves however they like. I think if people like chamber music or professional wrestling, that's fine, and surely that's why we have an extraordinarily wide variety of things people can do with their time. There are people who resent the attention and audience and enthusiasm slam poetry can provide, and so wind up saying derogatory things about it, or condescending things about it—e.g. I guess it's alright because maybe it will lead to the reading of true poetry the way Baptists feared that dancing might lead to sex. But there's nothing wrong with slam poetry, there's nothing wrong with doing crossword puzzles, there's nothing wrong with collecting old train schedules.

RL: Collecting butterflies?

WM: Nabokov liked it.

RL: Do you feel your work changing?

WM: Oh yes. My very first poems were the only ones I could write, short and imagistic. More contemplative and aphoristic asides of me needed me to develop more technical skill before I could voice them. A change in form means a change in content and vice versa (vice verse?). It's a snake whether you pick it up by its head or its tail.

Some changes have to do with will and boredom; viz., I'm so tired of writing blue poems I think I'll write some orange poems.

There are some changes that I suppose simply have to do with aging—our lives feel different to us at their successive stages, and they damn well should.

The older I get the less I like change and the more my poems seem to welcome it. And that makes sense, if symmetry is sense, for when I was younger wasn't I avid to change in ways my poems couldn't?

RL: But you do delve into the past for inspiration.

WM: The old axiom, you'll do it till you get it right is especially true in the arts. And you never will. There's inexhaustible energy in the past, especially in that part of the past that we separate out as childhood. But all the three tenses happen simultaneously in emotional life. You're always the past, you're always thinking about the future, and the tiny present is the hardest of the three tenses to inhabit, as it turns out.

But one's own artistic past is different. I always think of the publication party as being somewhat like the second half of a New Orleans funeral, the part where they turn their aprons around to the white side and play music all the way back into town from the cemetery. You have buried in fact that group of poems, and there's now an opportunity to use whatever energy is released by that for something else. So anything that invites you to go back and exhume that buried material is a bit of a confusion. Reading reviews of one's own work...

RL: ... and finally, which is your favorite deadly sin?

WM: Oh, that's hard to know. Where did this come up, in conversation recently? Oh, I know what it was. Two Sundays ago, or one, the Times Sunday crossword puzzle had seven clues which couldn't be completed without reference to one of the seven deadly sins. And I was talking about the crossword puzzle with a friend who was also doing it, which led to a discussion of which of the sins were the best. And I had little interest in sloth; I'm a worker. I guess gluttony and lust are the finalists for me. We'll see. I think if you live long enough gluttony wins, is perhaps how it works. But I'm not, I hope, close enough to the end to report on how that works

# MISCELLANY

# Last Lines:
# A Commonplace Book Constructed After the Fact

Literary Life

Early birds peck the lawn like myopic
typists. You have to get up damn early
in the morning not to moralize
nature, and it looks like I've overslept
again.

───

Q: What did you do when your heart got broken?
A: I fed wood to the fire, I read, I paced, I cleaned,
I sat and stared. Near dawn, raccoons, a family
on a field trip, skittered across the deck to peer
through five frank masks and plate glass at The Prince
of Garbage up late with his nerves and embers.

───

"My brother had every chance to keep his nose clean
but he blew it."

   *from a student paper*

───

Smoke Damage

No flour gets ground so fine, nearly liquid,
as this soot.

───

Q: What did the elephant ask the naked man?
A: How do you eat with that thing?

Stylish

"We'd all play like that if we could."
John Coltrane, of Stan Getz

A Wedding: His Fourth, Her Third

These two believe in the format.

Q: What did I forget to pack?
A: The antidote to coming back.

Curriculum Vitae

Post Toasties
Post Office
Post Dated
Post Partum
Postponement
Postponement
Post Mortem

*found on his desk the day after his death*

# AFTERWORD

# "To Learn to Love the Blues":
# William Matthews' *Search Party*
## Edward Byrne

> The most persistent theme in Matthews's poetry becomes that of temporality, the unyielding progression of time as it weakens one's abilities and eventually ends one's life, especially in dramatic or tragic instances where mortality shuts down the gifted artist.

The opening poem in a first collection of poetry by a young author often offers readers an introduction to favorite subjects or recurrent themes found throughout the larger body of work, presents insight into his or her main poetic concerns, poses for a moment while readers get a first glimpse or initial impression of the poet's persona as a character in his or her own poetry, and invites readers to the inaugural rendition of the poet's individual voice. In 1970, when William Matthews published his premiere book of poetry, *Ruining the New Road*, he began this volume with the curious, but correct choice of "The Search Party," a poem relating a night search by the speaker and other volunteers for a child lost in the wilderness. Walking "deep in symbolic woods" with lit flashlight and among "thick roots as twisted as / a ruined body," the poet addresses his "readers" and confides to them a concealed fear that he "might find something." As self-conscious as any speaker could be, a first-person narrator notes the obvious metaphor and irony contained in the process of telling the poem's story.

Indeed, the poet also foreshadows and explains his own repeated and actively involved presence—as actor, interpreter, or commentator—within the lines of a number of the poems in this collection: "I'm in these poems / because I'm in my life." By the close of the poem, the speaker even confronts the readers' awareness of this piece's perceived artificiality, particularly in its overt use of poetic devices, and the expectations that the tale, autobiographical or not, is really only a contrived form of art, not much more: "you're the one who thought it wouldn't / matter what we found." However, the clever poet knows better as he reveals in the final lines that, despite the poem's ominous imagery and potentially dangerous atmosphere painted with distinctly dramatic details, the child was found alive, and the speaker urges the readers, whom he imagines tense from the suspense of the situation, to confess a sense of relief at the outcome: "Admit you're glad."

With this introductory example, William Matthews quickly put forth for readers a brief and fairly precise indication of what kind of poetic qualities one might find not only in the rest of his first book, but moreso in much of his future production as a consequential American literary voice—as a confident and competent, yet ever-developing poet and analyst of poetry, whose work would mature even more fully, growing more complex in every subsequent volume over the next three decades. Already, a relaxed conversational voice, engaging each reader and speaking in a language filled with wit and self-reflexive wisdom, is in evidence, as is the appearance of the poet's candid and almost casual attitude, though certainly carefully considered and crafted, toward form with lines that at times resemble the improvisational grace notes one would witness in the live performances of those jazz musicians Matthews loved listening to and about which he frequently wrote.

Ironically, rather than undercutting the poem's power by raising the readers' level of attention to the artificiality of the poetic structure or eliminating the illusion of a shared experience between speaker and readers, except as common interpreters of the poem itself, the poet establishes an aesthetic distance that actually illuminates, more completely than a mere "flashlight's beam," a path beyond the individual incident of the lost child (and even the question of life or death for that one character in the poem) to some larger issues about artistic rendering of real-life events in a highly cynical postmodern era.

The poem subtly blurs a fine distinction between vision and re-vision or actual truth and authorial trust in the effectiveness of fictional pretense, between compositional tactics and contemplation of relayed facts, as the speaker suggests what matters most may truly be the readers' suspenseful expectations and emotional reactions to the perceived participants (poet and personae) and assumed actions in the poem rather than the course of direction in the fictitious chronicle of accounts chosen by the poet. The poem also initiates an ongoing exploration which will continue for Matthews throughout his career—the constant re-discovery of a tentative and evolving nature in the relationship (including its intrinsic characteristics of trust and credibility) which can develop between an artist and an audience simply by his insistence on investigating the elasticity of the limits, lyrical or narrative, existing in the extended monologue or implied dialogue a poet might pursue with the reader of any given poem.

Appropriately, "The Search Party" is once again the opening poem, as well as the title piece, for the latest compilation of William Matthews's poetry, a posthumous collection edited by his son, Sebastian Matthews, and good friend named literary executor of Williams's works, poet Stanley Plumly. Although the book's cover calls *Search Party* a volume of "Collected Poems," clearly that title can be misleading. As Plumly notes in the opening paragraph of the book's introduction, the poems included are meant only to "represent the best of William Matthews's ten original books of poetry," including *After All*, a collection submitted to his publisher by Matthews just days before his death by heart attack in 1997, as well as a selection of twenty-six poems previously uncollected in book form.

Plumly estimates that Matthews actually published "more than eight hundred poems" in magazines and literary journals: one hundred and sixty-five poems are gathered together in *Search Party*. In "My Father's Garden," an article by Sebastian Matthews that appeared in *Poets & Writers Magazine* and describes his efforts, along with others (Plumly, Peter Davison, and Michael Collier), to organize and release the many works—poetry and prose—that are part of William Matthews's literary history, the poet's son comments on the appropriation of the opening poem's title for the heading of this collection: "Through the editing process the four of us had become our own search party. We set out as a group to uncover my father's printed legacy. The treasures we found are collected in *Search Party*."

As is the case with most young poets, the poems chosen to represent *Ruining the New Road* hint at figures, contemporary or historical, whose own poetry influenced Matthews at that stage when his poetic voice was still developing. For instance, there are lines that seem to echo W.S. Merwin or Mark Strand and their books of that time period, Merwin's *The Lice* (1967) and Strand's *Darker* (1970), as well as Walt Whitman's *Leaves of Grass*. In addition, the selection from Matthews's first book includes a pair of poems—"Blues for John Coltrane, Dead at 41" and "Coleman Hawkins (d. 1969), RIP"—that are elegies for famous jazz musicians and foreshadow subject matter or themes that will appear numerous times over the next few decades. Indeed, if anything rivaled Matthews's passion for poetry, it was his devotion to music, especially the modern jazz that grew from the arrival of musicians who made their reputations in the mid-century bebop era, many whose music is referenced in the lines of Matthews's poems or whose names appear (rivaled only by the names of fellow poets) among the titles on *Search Party*'s table of contents: Coltrane, Hawkins, Bud Powell, Lester Young, Charles Mingus, etc.

Considering some of his comments on the relationship between poetry and music, one might even conclude music sometimes ranked higher for Matthews. In his essay titled "Poetry & Music," published in *The Poetry Blues* (2001), a posthumous anthology of Matthews's essays and interviews also edited by Sebastian Matthews and Stanley Plumly, he comments: "The power of music that poetry lacks is the ability to persuade without argument." In "Instrumental Bones," an interview with Matthews by Dave Johnson that also appears in *The Poetry Blues*, Matthews suggests the priority of music as an early influence in his life: ". . . music came first. We have rhythm before we have discourse."

The first three books of poetry by Matthews, published in the early seventies, display various influences of contemporary American poets at that transitional time of the sixties and seventies—Merwin, Strand, James Wright, Robert Bly, Charles Simic, Theodore Roethke—whose work often exhibited a style relying on surrealistic imagery and subjective voices. In his book of criticism, *Twentieth Century Pleasures*, Robert Hass remarks of James Wright that his collection, *The Branch Shall Not Break* (1963), may "have broken ground by translating the imagery of surrealist and expressionist poetics into American verse." This generation of "new surrealists" or "deep image poets" guided many younger poets toward a more associative and psychological imagery that might transform the ordinary into the extraordinary, might recognize the hidden revelations about the self lying underneath one's everyday surface existence.

Consequently, innovative and inventive images seemed to free the poet's imagination even more in ways similar to the opening of imagery that occurred in surrealist paintings. However, deep-image poems in their extreme, especially those that held severe brevity as a positive poetic characteristic, also appeared to lead toward a feeling of superficiality in the response of some readers. The emphasis almost solely on imagery allowed poets an opportunity to diminish the importance of subject matter, sometimes to an excess, seemingly avoiding any weighty themes as a matter of principle. As a result, a number of interesting, but ultimately insignificant poems were produced alongside the many remarkable pieces that have survived as signature poems of the period.

The selections in *Search Party* from the first three books by Matthews provide examples of these types of weaker works as well. For instance, *Sleek for the Long Flight* (1972) contains the following one-line poem, "The Needle's Eye, the Lens": "Here comes the blind thread to sew it shut." Another, slightly longer poem (a mere four lines in length) from the same collection is "Night Driving":

> You follow into their dark tips
> those two skewed tunnels of light.
> Ahead of you, they seem to meet.
> When you blink, it is the future.

By the time of the publication of *Rising and Falling* in 1979, William Matthews had arrived at a new, higher level in his writing of poetry. His main influences among contemporary poets seemed to shift from those who experimented with surrealist images towards those who promoted a more realistic description and more fully detailed account of the relationships between place and persona or between one's everyday exterior situations and one's understanding of the experiences which accompany them. Though not truly confessional nor strictly autobiographical writing, the poetry certainly was more concerned with subject matter and more transparently informed by specific recognizable elements of Matthews's autobiography. Matthews speaks of this in a 1997 interview with Peter Davison for *Atlantic Unbound* that also appears in *The Poetry Blues*: "I'm not a particularly autobiographical poet. There are circumstances and urges and emotions and quandaries and recurring problems that of course come through my work. I'm an autobiographical writer, therefore, to the extent that no writer can avoid being autobiographical, but I'm not a systematic and relentlessly autobiographical poet to the extent that, say, James Merrill was."

Matthews viewed his experiences—as a son or father, lover or husband, teacher or traveler, patient or caregiver, etc.—as resources for his poetry, situations that permitted him to engage and perceive life in a more enlightened or more insightful manner. In the same interview with Davison, Matthews concludes: "Life happens to us whether we have the good sense to be interested in the way it happens to us or not. That's what it means to be alive. Paying attention to it and trying to figure out what it does and doesn't mean (and what's wrong with seeking meaning in experience?)—these are opportunities."

In an interview with David Wojahn and James Harms recently released in the Fall, 2004 issue of *Blackbird*, Matthews observes, "there was subject matter that I was interested in writing about. A lot of the sort of Imagist/Deep Image poems were about the assumption that subject matter was a stand-in for something else." Later in the same interview, Matthews specifies some of the subjects on which he wanted to focus in his poetry, as he notes that in "the poems that start with *Rising and Falling*, which begin to include my sons and my domestic life, and so forth, much more than the earlier poems, there is a sense in which you're working out of very direct and practical concerns."

As Matthews chronicles in "Butterscotch Ripple," a chapter from *The Poetry Blues*, Richard Hugo had briefly become a colleague with Matthews at the University of Colorado in the mid-1970s and then a close friend until Hugo's death from leukemia in 1982. In an essay titled "Durations," which Matthews originally had written for the *Contemporary Authors Autobiography Series*, he speaks of the loss of Hugo: "Richard Hugo's death meant the loss of a good friend and one of my favorite poets." "Left Hand Canyon," one of the poems in *Rising and Falling*, is dedicated to Richard Hugo, and a few of the poems in this collection carry titles, highlighting place names, that resemble the ones Hugo used for his poetry and that he wrote of as "triggering towns" in his prose collection of lectures and essays on poetry writing.

Matthews also wrote the introduction to Hugo's posthumous collection of autobiographical essays, *The Real West Marginal Way: A Poet's Autobiography* (1986), in which Matthews claims all of Hugo's writing "is the work of ceaseless reclamation." Matthews expands: "It is to say along with Whitman that you can, by continuous imaginative appropriation, belong to America, however beautifully and terrifyingly vast it is. And it is to say that the continuous reclamation of a hometown, the original mystifying poise between self and others, is the lifelong imaginative project of any adult." Such a summary might be equally as pertinent in assessing most of the writings by William Matthews, especially those from *Rising and Falling* and afterwards.

The influence of Hugo and his poetry in the mid-seventies moved Matthews toward a more mature style of writing, one which appeared more frank and more revealing, one which included an even greater connection between the life lived and the lines of poetry derived from leading that life. Laurence Lieberman, writing of Hugo's poetry in his book of criticism, *Beyond the Muse of Memory*, has stated: "Many poems erupt with ardent impulsiveness, blurted messages phoned in haste and breathless passion from a noisy bar. The visitation has struck. Here. Now. You better listen, reader. Lover. This may be our only chance." Some of these characteristics of urgent address to the reader or others in the poet's life are also evident in the poems of *Rising and Falling*, as well as works that would follow in subsequent volumes.

Among the themes that seem to dominate *Rising and Falling*, as well as much of Matthews's later poetry, readers will find the classic contemplation by the poet on aging and meditation on mortality, the expected examination of life and death subjects; however, Matthews prefers to discuss time and the various consequences—physical, emotional, and spiritual—of its passing in a manner that requests readers look both backward and forward at the same time, see the connections, apparent or subconsciously contrived in their narratives, between one's childhood and the person one becomes in later life. In his book of criticism on contemporary poetry, *Local Assays*, Dave Smith describes the poetry in *Rising and Falling*: ". . . he wants to look quietly and speaks to us always like an intimate and avuncular friend. He intends to illuminate emotional time and space as well as their communal roots in memory. Meditation properly leads to a control of rising, falling breath; it means to slow down for suspended examination all that may be known or apprehended. Poetry, however, has to translate the apprehended into the tangible and Matthews makes a poem the art of the 'meditating mind.'" Matthews blends time periods in his life, often as a way to show one stage of growing is dependent upon another—or at least the perception of it one holds. Nothing should be viewed in isolation, no honest evaluation, even if informed by misremembered events or revised by recent recollections, would attempt to disconnect the boy from the man, the son from the father, or the apprentice poet from the master lyricist.

This section of *Search Party* begins with "Spring Snow," a poem whose title indicates a blending of time and a confusion of seasons. With most of the first three stanzas in this poem, Matthews describes ordinary events of his growing up as a typical Midwestern boy in Ohio; nevertheless, the images presented are themselves a blend, almost purely nostalgic scenes mixed with remembered details that provide a touch of impurity and cool just a bit the warmth of the memories, perhaps in a way similar to the spring weather and greening landscape now tainted by late snow. Stanley Plumly writes insightfully of this poem in "Chapter and Verse," a section from his book of criticism and commentary on poetry, *Argument & Song*: "The information is all Americana—from powdered milk to newspapers to spotted dog to the white laundry to the sheets. To rescue these memories from Norman Rockwell, Matthews punctuates them with qualification. The powdered milk saves money, the spotted dog is in heat, the sheets are watermarked with semen. Matthews is a master at redeeming the domestic cliché."

As is characteristic of Matthews's developing style and maturing poetic voice, after closing stanza three with a concluding statement ("Yet childhood doesn't end..."), a thesis that will become a continuing focus in future poems, "Spring Snow" goes on to more discursive language and abstract reflection in the lines of its final two stanzas:

> ... but accumulates, each memory
> knit to the next, and the fields
> become one field. If to die is to lose
> all detail, then death is not
>
> so distinguished, but a profusion
> of detail, a last gossip, character
> passed wholly into fate and fate
> in flecks, like dust, like flour, like snow.

In his interview with Wojahn and Harms, Matthews speaks of an evolving writing style during the period he was working toward completion of *Rising and Falling*. At the time, Matthews was dealing with divorce, relocation, and the relationships with his two sons, which forced him into "a more urgent, considerable curiosity about childhood." In "Moving Again," Matthews believes: "If I lived with my sons / all year I'd be less sentimental / about them."

Matthews hints at how he wished to use specific subjects as central points around which he could wind some twines of thought the way one might thread together associations and illuminations in a private late-night discussion with an old friend. In some instances, the language of a poem's lines might resemble words spoken at another personal moment, perhaps as if said during an intimate conversation with a lover. Matthews reveals, "at that point I was beginning to figure out that poems were a way of thinking. It seemed natural to want to write different kinds of poems under a different set of urgencies; and they very much had people in them and social consequences, and they were about different experiences with time; and they were about loyalty and betrayal."

The most persistent theme in Matthews's poetry becomes that of temporality, the unyielding progression of time as it weakens one's abilities and eventually ends one's life, especially in dramatic or tragic instances where mortality shuts down the gifted artist. In "Living Among the Dead," Matthews tells of once discovering furniture left by relatives who had died before he was born, and how he "opened two chests / of drawers to learn what the dead kept." Similarly, he suggests that literature, as with any art that freezes moments in life to preserve them long after the participants have passed, blends the past and present for its readers and painfully reminds all of our mortality even as it enriches our lives. Matthews reports, "it was when I learned to read / that I began always / to live among the dead." Commenting on "Living Among the Dead" in *Local Assays*, Dave Smith applauds how "Matthews examines his responsibility to ancestry, history, and artistry."

Likewise, the theme of temporality and an awareness of one's own mortality are both brought forth when one becomes a parent, witnesses the lives of one's children and contrasts their youth with one's own aging. Matthews knows responsibilities of the parent include sharing with them a knowledge of the past and of the dead: "To help his sons live easily / among the dead is a father's great work." At the same time, the presence of children and a life-affirming love for them assists the parent in his or her own dealings with mortality and death: "To love a child is to turn / away from the patient dead."

Nowhere are the issues of loss through death, as well as the temporality of one's ability to use talent, more distressingly apparent in Matthews's poetry than when it is pictured in conflict with the vitality of art, especially in his elegies for writers or musicians where readers realize that at the heart of such loss is the awakening to an additional absence, a void which involves the end of a magnificent creative spirit. Matthews begins "In Memory of W.H. Auden," a poem that honors one of his influences, with the following four lines: "His heart made a last fist. / The language has used him / well and passed him through. / We get what he collected." These poignant lines might also have served as an epigraph to *Search Party*.

*Rising and Falling* contains a pair of his patented poems mourning the passing of jazz greats who mattered so much to William Matthews: "Bud Powell, Paris, 1959" and "Listening to Lester Young." In the case of Bud Powell, his "hero," Matthews sees the painful end of that creative spirit even before Powell's physical death. As Powell's power is eroded by drug abuse, Matthews attends a performance in which the pianist's "white-water right hand clattered / missing runs nobody else would think / to try . . . ." In "Listening to Lester Young," pain and the approach of death are present once again:

> It's 1958, Lester Young minces
> out, spraddle-legged as if pain
> were something he could step over
> by raising his groin, and begins
> to play. Soon he'll be dead.

Young is "so tired / from dying he quotes himself, / easy to remember the fingering." The innovative spirit and incentive to invent new moves has been displaced by a desire to get by on what one has already done. There is nothing new or fresh, and the musician may already be stuck in his own past, imitating himself, rather than stepping forward into the future.

As noted above, such elegies for jazz musicians were written earlier in his career, including the previously mentioned "Blues for John Coltrane, Dead at

41" and "Coleman Hawkins (d. 1969), RIP" which appeared in his first book. However, with maturity has come a difference of perception for Matthews. In those earlier elegies, he tells the reader how he physically felt the deaths of these musicians. Hearing of Coltrane's death, he feels it in his feet, "as if the house were rocked / by waves from a soundless speedboat / planing by, full throttle." Upon learning of the death of Hawkins, Matthews writes:

> It's like having the breath
> knocked out of me
> and wearing the lost air for a leash.
> I snuffle home.
> I hate it that he's dead.

In both earlier elegies, Matthews tells the reader how he, too, felt pain with the passing of these men. However, in his later poems, rather than simply narrated, that pain is displayed in the poet's own actions, and a connection to time is made between past and present, or even to the future. Looking back in his poem about Bud Powell, Matthews notes: "I was young and pain / rose to my ceiling, like warmth, / like a story that makes us come true / in the present." In his homage to Lester Young which begins in 1958 and moves through 1976, Matthews concludes:

> It's 1976 and I'm listening
> to Lester young through stereo equipment
> so good I can hear his breath rasp,
> water from a dry pond—
> its bottom etched, like a palm,
> with strange marks, a language
> that was never born
> and in which palmists therefore
> can easily read the future.

The lessons learned from the music of these jazz masters, his heroes, and perhaps his tacitly identifying with them, may have been more instrumental than any other influence on Matthews's maturing voice. In "Instrumental Blues," his interview with Dave Johnson that appears in *The Poetry Blues*, Matthews acknowledges what his avid interest in modern jazz taught him as a poet: "There's something I know about phrasing and how to keep a fairly long sentence afloat for seven to a dozen lines of free verse without it losing its shape or momentum. If I'm right in thinking I can do that, I learned it more from listening to music than from listening to poetry."

Emotions associated with loss enter other poems from *Rising and Falling*, as Matthews's personal experiences affect his perspective and apparently alter his perceptions of the subjects in his poetry. In "Snow Leopards at the Denver Zoo," Matthews considers these nearly extinct animals ("only a hundred or so / snow leopards alive"), three of which the speaker watches as they jump inside their cages at the zoo, and he notices at the end of the first of two stanzas how the "snow / leopards land without sound, / as if they were already extinct." In the second stanza the speaker switches to a focus on himself, his concern for the leopards transitions to a contemplation of his own sense of loss and awareness of endangered aspects in his life: "If I tried to / take loss for a wife, and I do, / and keep her all the days of my life, / I'd have nothing to leave for my children."

Notably, in his introduction to *Search Party* Stanley Plumly isolates this poem for inspection as an example of Matthews's maturing voice in which "thought is not only feeling but a coherent language." Plumly correctly characterizes the tone of this poem and its positive attributes that will mark many of the poems in later poetry published by Matthews in books or in literary journals:

> The fragility of the poem is also its subject, the balance of saving "whatever I can keep" against the perishability of losing it all. Behind the poem is the certain knowledge —which is the theme in Matthews's poetry—that it will all, always, slip through our hands. This genius for turning the most familiar materials into something extraordinary— both smart and moving at once—comes from his gift for making connections and exploiting them to the limit their language will bear.

The mutual respect held for one another's poetry by Matthews and Plumly, as well as the likely influence on one another as poet and critic, is exemplified by the dedication to Plumly of "Long," the final poem in *Rising and Falling*. In "Chapter and Verse," Plumly—whose own outstanding breakthrough volume of poems, *Out-of-the-Body Travel*, had been published in 1977 exhibiting poetry Matthews held in high regard—outlines his admiration for the technical achievements in this "exceptional piece of work," a poem that again addresses death, loss, time, and memory:

> ... If we call the future's name
> it becomes our name, by echo.
>
> And from the dead, not even
> a plea that we leave them
> alone, each dead locked
> in its dead name.

Plumly singles out how this "extraordinary" poem "formulates rhetoric from ideas." He compliments the smooth movement of the poem, "as an entity." The unified nature of the connections in this poem seems to exhibit that established knack for phrasing and maintaining a lyric, line after line, "without it losing its shape or momentum" that William Matthews believed he had learned from listening to extended riffs of musicians in jazz clubs or on recordings. Plumly observes: "There are not even any images, in terms of the discrete. Instead, the poem reads as a single, self-sustaining 'image'—a fugue...."

Readers of *Rising and Falling* recognize the collection as a transformational volume, one in which the rhetoric of the surface language closely aligns with the deeper meaning of the poem until the two cooperate completely, almost inconspicuously combined as one. Plumly salutes Matthews's poem as "the condition of an idea, its music," and offers the following evaluation:

> This is free verse well in love with itself, free verse
> formalized and formulated so as to call attention to
> the discretion of its moves. The internal rhyming,

> the assonance, consonance, the soft touch on the
> alliteration—these are all clear enough. But
> underlining the overt technique is the pace of the
> sentences....

William Matthews followed *Rising and Falling* with the publication of *Flood* (1982), a collection that continued to treat those themes Matthews had adopted in his previous volumes of poetry. Once again, he revisits his childhood with a desire to revise memory, which he seems to distrust and by its nature most likely already exists in a revised form, to alter the past, consciously or not, simply by writing of it in the present and through time's filter. In the introduction to *Search Party*, Plumly points out the merit of Matthews's "quirky, often sardonic take on memory" that is displayed in a number of his poems. In "Housework," Matthews almost acts surprised or dismayed by what he finds when looking over his shoulders at his personal history, recalling a boyhood life in wonderfully lyrical lines:

> How you could have lived
> your boyhood here is hard to know,
> unless the blandishing lilacs
> and slant rain stippling the lamplight
> sustained you, and the friendship of dogs,
> and the secrecy that flourishes in vacant lots.

The speaker in the poem addresses the remembered persona of the boy with the second-person pronoun, as though the "you" were someone separate from the self of the adult speaker (the poet) and as if to emphasize both the differences in the lives led by the two and, eventually as he unites the pair in the final lines of the poem, the characteristics that are transferred through time from child to adult, shared by boy and man alike. Nevertheless, the speaker questions the authenticity of memory, limited as it is, and wonders whether the writer's ability to revise can actually re-create the conditions of the past in a manner more palatable to the poem's present persona by wiping clean the surface details, a type of housework, to ease his ongoing questioning of the effects of time.

Elsewhere in *Flood*, Matthews concludes "Cows Grazing at Sunrise" with a specific question about time and memory, about what our concept of the "past" really entails when we attempt to remember it: "And isn't the past inevitable, / now that we call the little / we remember of it 'the past'?" In "School Figures," Matthews describes the pre-dawn practice of a skater cutting figure eights over and over into a fresh ice surface, circling backwards to see where she has been and to measure her success or failure. The speaker seems to be commenting as much on poetry, when he offers his observation:

> So much learning is forgetting
> the many mistakes for the few
> lines clear of the flourishes
> you thought were style, but were
> only personality, indelible as
> it seemed.

By the time the poem ends, the speaker has concluded "learning and forgetting / are one attention," and that is the interest which repeatedly draws the subject, this figure skater, to each pre-dawn practice, "turning / over your shoulder as if you could / skate back into your first / path and get it right for once." Again, looking back to the past, time after time, for guidance on how to proceed in the future seems on the surface to be a wise maneuver, but the words "as if" suggest the speaker in the poem feels such moves will ultimately prove futile.

In an essay from *The Poetry Blues*—"Merida, 1969," titled after one of his poems—that Matthews originally wrote for an anthology (*Ecstatic Occasions, Expedient Forms*, edited by David Lehman) in which poets comment on the composition of one of their own works, he speaks of the connection his view of the past and memory, as they are presented in poems or stories, seems to have with Robert Frost's "The Road Not Taken." As in Frost's well-known poem, Matthews believes many of his pieces that regard the past, relying on one's often faulty and usually self-serving memory of long ago incidents, are works that alter the actual events. Matthews indicates that, even if an autobiographical moment is related in a poem, what happened in real life is bound to be re-shaped by the speaker telling the poem or story. In the example of Frost's poem: "The roads beckoned about the same, but later, when the pleasure of telling the story was part of the story's truth, and there was much intervening life to explain, we could hear the poem's speaker veer off again, this time away from incident and toward shapeliness."

Matthews's own reluctance to rely on the past and his distrust of memory for accuracy or factual truth, especially in the direction or the details of his poems, are explained when he notes Frost's speaker's famous false final lines, already disproved by previous details in the poem: "I took the one less traveled by, / And that has made all the difference." Matthews reports the speaker as "giving his little anecdote a neat and summary dramatic effect that's in the story but not in the original event. Though of course by this stage in the life of the story each exists somewhat for the sake of the other." In his poem, Matthews proposes two versions of the truth—what happened and what might have occurred "if we'd been happy / then, as now we often are." About the changes his own poem consciously forces onto the facts of the actual events with friends that inspired the work, Matthews confesses: "In this second and hypothetical life, they may or may not be wiser, but they are happier...."

The last pair of poems ("Nabokov's Death" and "On the Porch at the Frost Place, Franconia, NH") from *Flood* pay homage to two writers—Vladimir Nabokov and Robert Frost—who, like Matthews, enjoyed including shadowy figures juxtaposed against situations representing the lighter side of life. (Also, the second of the poems offers an additional nod to Stanley Plumly, to whom Matthews once more dedicates his poem.) Nabokov knew readers were willing to accept the darker parts of his fiction amid its wit and humor because "we'll hold to our grief, / stern against grace, because we love / a broken heart." Matthews shares some of Nabokov's attitude toward the audience for his art, and he approves of Nabokov's playful way of manipulating reality in the tricks of his fiction, how he was a writer who delighted in eventually inviting the readers to participate by letting them in on the deception, displaying the artifice: "he loved the art that reveals art / and all its shabby magic."

Matthews recognizes the important influence of Robert Frost. He respects Frost's poetry for its "disguises" consisting of deliberate deception and ambiguity, the way it sometimes illuminates a subject indirectly or from different perspectives, as if its surface maintains a multiple of cut angles with facets reflecting surrounding light. He seems to appreciate the demands Frost places on his readers to participate and be as willing to face their darker sides even when a more amenable meaning might be available:

> So here the great man stood,
> fermenting malice and poems
> we have to be nearly as fierce
> against ourselves as he
> not to misread by their disguises.

Like Matthews, Frost was capable of lulling his readers with a comfortable conversational tone while at the same time challenging those same readers to discover the more disturbing or dismaying elements camouflaged by a soothing or reassuring poetic voice. Even when images are conveyed through lyrical language, these two poets know how to ask readers to confront difficult questions about their own everyday conditions as human beings whose lives contain conflicts or decisive moments with possibly dire consequences hanging in the balance that might evoke emotions of uncertainty, sadness, regret, and grief, among others. Matthews summarizes: "... Frost's great poems, / like all great poems, conceal / what they merely know, to be / predicaments."

Death, absence, and memory, three of the primary elements necessary for elegy, persist in *A Happy Childhood*, published by Matthews in 1984. The crucial title poem of this collection demonstrates how unmistakably ambitious and complex his poetry had become as he moved further from the deep images or more surrealist touches in his earlier work. Much of the subject matter and language is deceptively ordinary and plain in "A Happy Childhood"; yet, the content and the breadth of the poem's emotional range represent a lifelong consideration of one's past and an accumulation of deep personal associations made in meditation upon that past. In his autobiographical memoir of 1994, "Durations," Matthews attempted to retrieve the conditions surrounding his earliest memory in the back yard of his grandmother's Iowa home, but he retains only a fragmented set of details in his recollection of the scene: "a sandbox, a tiny swatch of grainy sidewalk, and—there! it's moving—a ladybug." Out of these bits from the farthest parcels of his memory, Matthews desired to manufacture a factual story, to fill in the missing blanks. However, as much as he might try, he believed he was unsuccessful in his prose account: "I have tried again and again to construct a tiny narrative from these bright props, but they won't connect. They lie there and gleam with promise but won't connect."

Nevertheless, when Matthews turns his attention to the same subject matter in his poetry, he proves much more successful because he can make connections without seeking the continuous and chronological narrative the prose of his memoir would demand. Instead, the form chosen for "A Happy Childhood" consists of more than fifty three-line stanzas subtly set off in four sections signaled only by an extra white space placed between stanzas. The poem opens with an autobiographical recollection involving an example of his mother's sense of humor, the type of wit he admired, as she uses literary allusion to command the family dog into the yard with the comment, "Out out damn Spot." Already, a past personal moment blends with a reference to writing as "A Happy Childhood" delivers a message about reverence for the influence of memory and an instilled love for literature. The poem also preserves an elegiac tone that now hovers over everything:

> I hate it when anyone dies or leaves and the air
> goes slack around my body and I have to hug myself,
> a cloud, an imaginary friend, the stream in the road-
> side park.

The emotion of anger expressed here is echoed later in "An Elegy for Bob Marley"—another poetic tribute to a musician, this time a reggae legend—where Matthews determines: "Surely the real fuel for elegy / is anger to be mortal." Thus, the poetic declarations of pain and sorrow over the loss of another in elegies are often more revelatory of the frustrations and fears their emotionally affected speakers feel. They expose how vulnerable we all are in our everyday existence, a condition most hope to ignore a majority of the time. However, they especially remind us of the fragility of life when we are forced to face evidence of our own mortality in the images of others' deaths, especially when the treasured voice or vision of an artist, someone who has enriched our lives or with whom we have identified, is ended as well.

Connections between the present and the past or future weave together the various stages in one's life, each influencing the other. One incident in "A Happy Childhood" is labeled "a memory in the making." Later, a boy in the poem "goes home to memory." The poet then elevates the act of remembering as he nearly reveres memory and speaks in veneration of it when he compares memory to prayer. Individuals, similar to their memories, continually undergo change and are altered by the way their present portrays the past or is explained by the past. Matthews proposes: "It turns out you are the story of your childhood / and you're under constant revision." In fact, our perceptions of the past as viewed through memory are so transformed throughout time that our lives may become nothing other than the stories we tell ourselves and those we know, little more than renditions that try to depict who we have been and, ultimately, how we will be remembered even by those closest to us when we are gone. The past and our personalities constitute a compilation of remembered experiences, and memories can, often do, differ between even those who share the same situations. Such a contrast occurs in the memories of mother and son in this poem:

> He'll remember like a prayer
> how his mother made breakfast for him
>
> every morning before he trudged out
> to snip the papers free. Just as
> his mother will remember she felt
>
> guilty never to wake up with him
> to give him breakfast. It was Cream
> of Wheat they always or never had together.

Poet or not, each person authors and revises his or her own story that defines a life. We often depend upon tentative or unreliable memories in constructing the stories that identify us. In "Durations," Matthews observes that his earliest memories may be his own, or the repeated details of relatives' anecdotes, or a blend of these that mixes "like vodka slipped into a bowl of punch." In the end, though, we are responsible for the fact combined with fiction in the narratives of our lives. We possess a power that allows us to steer a clear direction toward personal definition:

> There's no truth about your childhood,
> though there's a story, yours to tend,
>
> like a fire or garden. Make it a good one,
> since you'll have to live it out, and all
> its revisions, so long as you shall live. . . .

At gatherings of writers and readers or among members of associations formed to promote literature, William Matthews was a well-known personality whose public persona and personal behavior often drew attention, for better or for worse. His service as an officer in literary organizations included terms as president in the Poetry Society of American and in the Associated Writing Programs. He also participated as both a member and as a chair of the National Endowment for the Arts Literature Panel. In addition, Matthews was widely recognized as a teacher of creative writing at various universities, including Cornell University, the University of Colorado, the University of Washington, and City College of New York, among others.

Sometimes, Matthews's seemingly reckless and self-destructive personal behavior trespassed upon his living as a college professor and his livelihood as a poet. Although Matthews rarely permitted his poetry to reach the point where it might be viewed as "confessional"—and never allowed his work to completely drift toward the more confessional mode of Robert Lowell or Sylvia Plath—as *A Happy Childhood* suggests, autobiographical elements almost always influenced his writing in one way or another, particularly in later volumes of his poetry. When Matthews published *Foreseeable Futures* in 1987, he had "just come through the most difficult passage" of his life, according to his son, Sebastian, who wrote a memoir titled *In My Father's Footsteps* (2004), released in the same year as *Search Party*. Matthews had left his position as holder of Roethke Chair in creative writing at the University of Washington under a cloud of scandal and accusations. His reputation as a professor had been damaged by widespread stories that raised questions concerning his behavior toward women, especially his relationships with female students.

Sebastian Matthews reports his father's troubles in the memoir. He relates how his father was confronted with official university charges and a filed lawsuit from a female student with whom he had an affair, suggesting the charges perhaps had been leveled by the young woman as a measure of revenge for the unpleasant ending of the relationship. Sebastian Matthews wonders why his father repeatedly risked such a highly-respected position at the university by engaging in a series of affairs with his students. "I know that he couldn't stop himself. Was he a sex addict? A compulsive womanizer? I don't know," writes the son. The trial eventually concluded without a verdict by a hung jury, and the charges were not pursued further; however, by then William Matthews had moved across the country to New York City.

In "Durations," Matthews recalls how throughout his youth "New York had been the preferred weekend destination from boarding school and then from college." He had come "for the museums and especially for the jazz clubs." With its easy access to the great jazz clubs (even though some from his college days were no longer open) and a magnificent opera house, with the numerous restaurants and cultural centers, and with a new wife—someone who had been in publishing and wrote psycholanalytical books, and a woman who seemed to have a settling affect on him—Matthews gradually found himself at home in a Manhattan apartment and comfortable with a teaching position at City College.

Sebastian Matthews speaks of *Foreseeable Futures* in his book:

> There are no out-and-out love poems in *Foreseeable Futures*, the 1987 book that my father dedicated to Arlene. I am not sure there needs to be. The whole book is a love poem of sorts—a toast raised to a life, if not always well lived, then at least survived with grace. Throughout its pages, I see my father breathing a sigh of relief, as if looking around and

appreciating the small ironies. He's just come through the most difficult passage of his adult life, and he's still standing. Not only that, but he's found a new partner, a great apartment in his beloved city; he's got work, a new book out, friends around him. His sons have grown up, gone off not to prison but college. Things are truly looking up.

Although not one of his stronger collections, *Foreseeable Futures* contains poems that slip to readers a few glimpses at the attitude toward self Matthews may have had in moments of reflection during his mid-forties and at such a turning point in his life. "It feels like the very middle, the exact / fulcrum of our lives," he writes in "April in the Berkshires." Matthews often spoke or wrote in a self-deprecating manner about himself and any emotional or physical shortcomings he believed he exhibited, such as his lanky build and the way clothes crumpled over his frame or the athletic limits set by his body, especially his knees gnarled from the "thousands of hours of driveway and playground basketball" ("Durations"). Remarking wittily of private resentment he feels toward his poet persona (the public self others perceive) in "The Complaint," a brief essay included in *The Poetry Blues*, Matthews declares: "I'm very emotional and easily filled with formless murk, and sometimes I get weepy like this, I'm sorry. Yes, thank you. He's glib, he files his tongue before he brushes his teeth, and he's diligent as a dog." Matthews also includes himself among those he terms "Fellow Oddballs" in a poem by that title from *Foreseeable Futures*:

> ... Here's to us,
> morose at dances and giggly in committee,
>
> and here's to us on whose ironic bodies new clothes
> pucker that clung like shrink wrap to the manikins.
> And here's to the threadbare charm of our self-pity.

One of the more powerful poems ("The Accompanist") in this collection offers Matthews an opportunity to make another connection between poetry and music. Many times in interviews and essays Matthews displays admiration for—even identification with—the musicians who accompanied the great female jazz vocalists, like Lester Young with Billie Holiday or Louis Armstrong with Bessie Smith. "I have certain dopey identifications with Lester Young, it's true. There's a combination in Young of strong emotion, not so much concealed as released by diffidence, irony, and sweetness of tone, that doesn't sound far off from certain textures in my poems, unless my ear is off," Matthews told Sascha Feinstein in "Mingus at the Showplace," an interview from *The Poetry Blues*.

Sebastian Matthews comments on the opening lines of "The Accompanist" ("Don't play too much, don't play / too loud, don't play the melody."): "I can't help picturing Tommy Flanagan here, talking about his years with Ella Fitzgerald. Or Mal Waldron in an interview about backing Billie. Or maybe it's the poet himself, hiding behind a persona, who is speaking so wisely about the exact difficulties (and rewards) of writing—and living—well." In "The Accompanist," Matthews surely appears to be drawing a parallel between the subtlety of a jazz musician accompanying the compelling content and delivery of a singer's lyrics—it's "her story"—and the way a poet's lyricism sharpens or soothes (as much as it reflects the world his words might reveal), both records and consoles at the same time, and maybe even hints at levels beneath the surface, toward those acts in the life of the artist to which the poetic lines might allude or that certain words may indirectly portray, but left mostly unmentioned in any overt way:

> . . . When you play it you become
> your part in it, one of her beautiful
> troubles, and then, however much music
> can do this, part of her consolation,
> the way pain and joy eat off each other's
> plates, but mostly you play to drunks,
> to the night, to the way you judge
> and pardon yourself, to all that goes
> not unsung, but unrecorded.

By the time *Blues If You Want* was released in 1989, William Matthews had experienced the end of his second marriage, and the tone of the poems contained in this volume shifts once again. His voice sounds as assured, yet unassuming as in any of his collections. The works show a sense of confidence and control even when their content poses questions the poet cannot answer or creates quandaries that he cannot resolve. The images are sometimes darker and the wit sharper than in his previous poetry. In considering differing aspects of subject matter, Matthews brings together his varying topics of interest (music, literature, language, travel, memory, love, and loss, among others) with as much success as he'd ever done in one book of poems.

This book filled with the color blue seemingly appearing in nearly every poem or with titles alluding to "blue"—such as "Nabokov's Blues," "Mood Indigo," "The Blues," and "Little Blue Nude"—and evoking emotional blues, Matthews gives the reader a glimpse into this blue period of his life. In "The Blues," Matthews traces the connections between music and mood, and he suggests ways for the reader to view conditions of loneliness or loss. In a time of sorrow, those musicians Matthews admired so much now provided a needed companionship and a complementary sense of expression, empathy for the status of the spirit: ". . . I knew the way music can fill a room, / even with loneliness, which is of course a kind / of company."

By the close of this poem, Matthews discovers an approach to the future that he has been wanting ever since he was a boy. As he states, it is "the future toward which I clatter / with that boy tied like a bell around my throat, // a brave man and a coward both, / to break and break my metronomic heart / and just enough to learn to love the blues."

In "Nabokov's Blues," Matthews defines an aspect of the pain one might find at a troubled time of life:

> This is the secret ache that hurts most, the way
> desire burns bluely at its phosphorescent core:
>
> just as you're having what you wanted most,
> you want it more and more until that's more
> than you, or it, or both of you, can bear.

Matthews even sees the beauty in various shades of blues, "every hue and tint," one might view through an evening in the end of summer. In "Moonlight in Vermont" he summarizes:

> There's no illusion here.
> It's beautiful to watch
> and that's reason enough for blue after blue
> to blossom, for each decaying swatch
>
> to die into the next. The faster it goes
> the less hurry I'm in for home or anywhere.

Matthews eventually recognizes associations with "unspent love" and the lateness of the hour as he observes:

> By now the moon itself is blue. By this
> we mean that we can see in it the full freight
> of our unspent love for it, for the blue night,
> and for the hour, which is late.

Perhaps the most revealing poem in *Blues If You Want* is one that addresses the poet's reactions after discovering his apartment has been robbed while he was away in Tennessee. Matthews knows the identity of the burglar, "Tony, my dumpster-diving friend," whose girlfriend the poet had comforted recently after she'd been beaten by Tony. Matthews declares even a robbery is "designed to hurt," to take away those things one loves most, as the thief—to whom Matthews had previously confided about his jazz tapes, "I just love these"—steals a tape deck, but leaves behind the poet's typewriter. Perceptively, the thief discerns Matthews's apparent preference for the language of Ben Webster over the words of Merriam-Webster. The poet concludes: "Writing's my scam, he thought, and music my love." The speaker in the poem explains the elevated place of music in his life:

> . . . you could turn to music you love, not as mood-
> altering drug nor as a consolation, but because
> your emotions had overwhelmed and tired you
> and made you mute and stupid, and you rued
>
> them every one. But then Webster kicks into
> his first chorus, they're back, all your emotions,
> every one, and in another language, perhaps
> closer to their own.

Matthews recalls all this in retrospect, when he arranges the continuity of his thoughts and sorts his emotions through the composed and controlled, though contrived, clarity of memory; as Matthews also admits "afterthought" to be "the writer's specialty and curse." In the face of loss, Matthews muses that one of the marvels of living is "how much we manage to hang on to."

The final stanza of "Little Blue Nude" presents Matthews's eventual response to a neighbor's question concerning the new book the poet is writing. "What's it about?" Matthews is asked. Matthews acknowledges he didn't know how to reply then, and he didn't even ask himself "until later." However, he ultimately concludes this poem with an answer that accurately characterizes not only *Blues If You Want*, but much of his other work as well: "It's a reverie on what I love, and whom, / and how I manage to hold on to them."

Upon the release of *Blues If You Want* in 1989, William Matthews planned a publication celebration scheduled so his parents could attend while in the United States. The day following the book party, his parents returned to England where "his father had a massive heart attack at the luggage retrieval area in the Newcastle upon Tyne airport," Matthews records in "Durations." Further, Matthews notes in this essay published just prior to the release of his next collection of poems (*Time and Money*, which won the National Book Critics Circle Award), he was reminded how deeply he'd been affected by the loss of others since his grandfather's death. He reviews the strong reactions he'd especially had to the passing of artists, writers, and musicians, evident ever since his earlier works. Matthews writes: "I've seen the deaths of writers and musicians who'd meant as much to me as family members—Thelonius Monk, Charles

Mingus, Vladimir Nabokov, Elizabeth Bishop. In the case of artists like these, whose continued development and invention had produced not only beloved work but a model for the way a life in the arts can be imagined and lived out, the deaths meant an absolute end to the marvelous momentum by which an important body of work is produced."

Matthews realizes in "Durations" his enhanced awareness of mortality, heightened by the death of his father and by witnessing his own sons grow into adulthood, even making him a grandfather: "I have never been more aware that the meter is running and, consequently, never been more vivid, concentrated, happy, or warily hopeful."

Nevertheless, *Time and Money* contains a number of references to grief and sorrow, depression and loss. Time is described as a primary cause of much of the pain we feel, an element that creates sadness in our lives and the lives of those we love, and then takes away those lives. One of the title poems, "Time," questions whether "time's just one more inexact way / to gauge loss." However, Matthews follows with a reminder that memory and the lessons learned through time, and perhaps the stilled moment in an artist's work, allow us to "keep more than we think." Matthews advises:

> To begin thinking about time, we might
> take all the verbs we like to think we do
> to time, and turn those verbs on us, and say
> that time wastes us, and time saves and buys us,
> that time spends us, and time marks and kills us.

Matthews has learned to cope with the passage of time and the erosion ("water licks its steady way through stone") it inflicts ("my male friends my age and I / scan the obits every day. The word / 'time' now seems, often enough, the nickname / for the phrase 'time left.'") Through writing poetry, the art that has served him so well, he connects the past to the present even more: "Now critics write / of my 'mature work.'" Matthews appears to explain one purpose for his composition of poetry, an activity that provides a way to confront, and maybe control, fear of what the future holds:

> I'd soldier through
> the fear and depressions. I'd call on
> what those critics like nicely to call 'wit,'
> i.e., the whole compressed force of my rage
> and love. I'd invent whatever it took
> to get me through or dead, whichever came
> first.

In a couple of poems Matthews directly addresses the death of his father and the absence left behind. The movement of time ages us all and in time we are taken away. Matthews begins "My Father's Body": "First they take it away, / for now the body belongs to the state. / Then they open it / to see what may have killed it. . . ." After death and the scattering of the ashes, what remains of the father Matthews knew, "a mild, democratic man / will sift in a heap with the residue of others, / for now they all belong to time."

The recognition of mortality and fear of death Matthews experiences is magnified in the minds of the men of his father's generation, those he believed closer to losing their own battles with time. Matthews observes this among the mourners he meets in "Men at My Father's Funeral": "The ones his age who shook my hand / on their way out sent fear along / my arm like heroin." As always, Matthews responds to the unsettling of his own emotions through the use of language:

> And I, the glib one, who'd stood
> with my back to my father's body
> and praised the heart that attacked him?
> I'd made my stab at elegy,
> the flesh made word: the very spit
>
> in my mouth was sour with ruth
> and eloquence.

Throughout his poetry, William Matthews imaginatively wrestles with the past—how it influences and shapes the present, but also how even the faulty memory of the past is influenced and shaped by the present. Yet, Matthews knows he can never fully or accurately hold on to time, or hold it back; instead, the true nature of the past escapes even the artist who wishes to preserve it, to keep alive the moments of the past and those who lived those moments.

Nevertheless, perhaps it is enough to know we experienced what now may exist only in unreliable memories or fictional memoirs. In "Note Left for Gerald Stern in an Office I Borrowed and He Would Next, at a Summer Writers' Conference," Matthews concludes the poem with words offered from one poet to another, and shared as well with the reader: "And then we're back, alone / not with the past but with how fast the past / eludes us, though surely, friend, we were there."

In addition to how Time measures various forms of erosion in our lives, the focus on Money in this collection of poetry also directs the reader toward ways to gauge emotional evolution and explore more closely how we account for ourselves, whether one examines love, loss, or other feelings we experience. In "Money" Matthews asks:

> What do
> we want, and how much will we pay
> to find out, and how much never to know?
> What's wrong with money is what's wrong with love:
>
> it spurns those who need it most for someone
> already rolling in it.

Just as Matthews tries to unravel the twisted and tangled threads of time, he also hopes to show how the material nature of money may calculate the cost of living, the price we pay day after day:

> Money's not an abstraction; it's math
> with consequences, and if it's a kind
> of poetry, it's another inexact way,
> like time, to measure some sorrow we can't
> name.

At the time of William Matthews's death in 1997, he had finished a new collection of poetry. That manuscript, *After All*, was released in 1998 and, as he had done in the past, he delights readers with his wry humor in poems like "Oxymorons"—a work that gathers together clusters of phrases, figures of speech with seemingly self-contradictory words in various areas, including "money's . . . rich in such mischief." Appropriately, Matthews closes this poem with another glance at the topic of human memory: "Our memories / will be our *real estate*, all that we've got."

Nevertheless, *After All* continues to display some of the darker themes and the somber emotional tone detected in much of *Time and Money*. Indeed, had readers not come upon similar poems in earlier works, they may have been startled by the way Matthews again depicts time's erosion of body and spirit. Matthews once more addresses mortality and the helpless feelings of frustration, fear, and anger that often accompany one's confrontation with aging and a weakening physical condition, whether it be oneself or another one admires and loves who is the subject of such deterioration and who faces the prospect of death. As an example, Matthews begins "Mingus in Shadow":

> What you see in his face in the last
> photograph, when ALS had whittled
> his body to fit a wheelchair, is how much
> stark work it took to fend death off, and fail.

Even the name of this final collection seems to hint toward an ending and an exhaustion as one looks backwards at what has been experienced or endured during a lifetime. Sebastian Matthews writes in his introductory note to *The Poetry Blues*: "My father died having just completed a manuscript of poems. The book, prophetically titled *After All*, was already sitting on the desk of his editor, Peter Davison."

The book's title fits nicely the attitude of the speaker who regards that last photograph of Charles Mingus and concludes that after all the musician had suffered, physically and emotionally, and even now after death, the music and memories that remain are most important, provide a light in dark times. Matthews had confessed in his interview with Sascha Feinstein ("Mingus at the Showplace") to having "the most complicated relationship to Mingus. I set that up for myself rather deliberately. Call it hero worship, call it role model... I picked him as a tutelary figure."

In addition, one could claim "to take the photograph" is also an act of taking the spirit represented by the one in the picture, taking it from the grasp of time and preserving it in a timeless portrait. The image in the photograph, itself a form of art, serves as a perfect metaphor of the human endeavor and those aspects, especially the gifts to others that are represented in the performances or works created throughout an artist's life, that are maintained in the minds of those left behind:

> It was human nature,
> tiny nature, to take the photograph,
>
> to fuss with the aperture and speed, to let
> in the right blare of light just long enough
> to etch pale Mingus to the negative.
> In the small, memorial world of that
> negative, he's all the light there is.

Matthews compactly summarizes much of his understanding of the atmosphere he'd found around him in his personal circumstances in "Care":

> Books get read and written.
> My mother comes to visit. My father's
>
> dead. Love needs to be set alight
> again and again, and in thanks
> for tending it, will do its very
> best not to consume us.

Certainly, this book of William Matthews's poetry should be read by anyone who desires to comprehend the cumulative impact of his poems, three decades in the making, and to better seize the self that was William Matthews. In "Privacies," an essay from *The Poetry Blues*, Matthews explains "the world inside the reach of our wishes, the self, is the world we mostly live in, if only because we have small power in the other, the one we casually call the 'real' world. And in that inner world, where we mostly live, poetry and its allies—prayers, curses, sexual fantasies and other daydreams, letters, diaries, and all the other members of the chorus—make the music, like an internal weather, to which everything happens." Throughout his life, William Matthews admired, idolized, and identified with the great jazz musicians of his time, and in the lines of his poetry he learned how to make his own music "to which everything happens."

In "A Poetry Reading at West Point," responding to questions about his poetry, the speaker reveals a personal assessment of what he attempts to achieve when composing his poems: "I try to write as well as I can / what it feels like to be human." Likewise, readers of *Search Party* will find what they are seeking as they recover what it feels like to be human—including the faults, frailties, fears, and failures, but also the tenderness, tenacity, truths, and triumphs—and readers will be rewarded with the re-discovery of the poet who in his poems opened up his personality, which included all of those characteristics and more, the human who was William Matthews.

# Biographical Notes

**WILLIAM MATTHEWS** won the National Book Critics Circle Award in 1995 and the Ruth Lilly Award of the Modern Poetry Association in 1997. Born in Cincinnati in 1942, educated at Yale University and the University of North Carolina, Matthews taught and lectured all over the United States. At of the time of his death in 1997, he was a professor of English and Director of the writing program at the City University of New York. In his lifetime, Matthews authored of over a dozen books of poetry and prose, including *Search Party: Collected Poems of William Matthews* (Houghton Mifflin).

**SEBASTIAN MATTHEWS** is the author of the poetry collection *We Generous* (Red Hen Press) and a memoir, *In My Father's Footsteps* (W. W. Norton). He co-edited, with Stanley Plumly, *Search Party: Collected Poems of William Matthews*. Matthews teaches at Warren Wilson College and serves on the faculty at Queens College Low-Residency MFA in Creative Writing. Matthews serves on the editorial board of Q Ave Press, makers of handmade poetry chapbooks.

**STANLEY PLUMLY** has written nine books of poetry, including *Out-of-the-Body Travel*, which was nominated for a National Book Critics Circle Award, and *Now That My Father Lies Down Beside Me, New and Selected Poems, 1976 - 2000*. He has recently published a collection of essays, *Argument & Song*, the "personal" biography *Posthumous Keats*, and, most recently, *Old Heart: Poems*.